William J Fay

LOVE COMMANDS IN THE NEW TESTAMENT

Pheme Perkins

PAULIST PRESS
New York/Ramsey

Library of Congress
Catalog Card Number: 82-80157

ISBN: 0-8091-2450-5

Published by Paulist Press
545 Island Road, Ramsey, N.J. 07446

Printed and bound in the
United States of America

CONTENTS

A Note to the Reader

This book developed out of the Bible lectures, which I was invited to give at Bethel College, North Newton, Kansas, on Feb. 15–17, 1981. They can now see why I was always rushing to get all the material in during each lecture! The Mennonite tradition has a strong sense of the obligations of Christian community, and the Bethel community was a most hospitable and appreciative audience. My thanks to all the people who made my stay at Bethel an enjoyable one, especially those who were in charge of seeing that I wound up in the right places at the right time—Prof. Perry Yoder, Rev. John Esau, and Mrs. Hilda Voth. No wonder Dorothy was so persistent in her efforts to find the Wizard and get back home to Kansas!

I would also like to thank my colleague at Boston College, Prof. Lisa Cahill, who persistently asks me to make all this New Testament exegesis available for the reflection of the Christian ethicist. Exegetes all need to be blasted out of the "biblical world" occasionally! I presume that this book will merely start more of those conversations at the office door.

Finally, I would ask the reader to take seriously the suggestions about studying the biblical passage before reading each chapter. A book about the Bible should never become a substitute for the Bible itself. The small amount of time invested in discovering the biblical text before beginning the analysis in each chapter will pay large dividends in understanding. The Study Questions at the end of each chapter will help you summarize your understanding of its content.

INTRODUCTION
The Problem of a New Testament Ethic

The Cultural Setting of New Testament Ethics

Some people wonder whether it is possible to speak of a New Testament ethic as a basis for ethical decision-making in the twentieth century. They point out that New Testament writings accept without question such social features of first century life as slavery and subjection of women, which many Christians today feel must be rejected. We also know that in the centuries immediately after the New Testament was written Christians were quite content to argue that the "love command" did not make Christianity different or ethically superior to other traditions. Rather, it showed that Christianity embodied the highest ideals of philosophical wisdom, a universal charity or love of humanity [Whittaker]. This attitude suggests that Christians were not concerned to distinguish themselves from their cultural milieu on ethical grounds. Indeed, within the New Testament itself we see that both Jesus and the New Testament writers draw heavily on the ethical traditions of the Old Testament, of common wisdom traditions, and of the Hellenistic ethical codes generally to address concrete situations. They do not attempt to elaborate a special "system" of Christian ethics.

One of the more distinctive features of many of the New Testament writings is the expectation that the final judgment is near. Jesus is going to return soon and condemn all who do evil. This expectation led people to focus on the individual perfection of members of the community. They wanted to be sure of salvation when the Lord returned. But it also led to a lack of concern for the larger questions

of social and political justice. Since all those structures were about to
be abolished, it was possible to give slaves and others the "let it be
for now," "endure patiently" advice that appears so often in New
Testament writings. Such an outlook can hardly be the basis for
Christian action in an on-going world.

New Testament Ethics as the "Critical Edge"

The questions raised by consideration of the relationship between the New Testament ethic and its cultural setting remind us
that we cannot study any ethical teaching in the New Testament
without looking very carefully at how that teaching would have appeared in its own time. Jesus and his disciples did not have to "invent
ethics." They lived within the religious tradition of Judaism, which
had a long history of ethical reflection in both the law of Moses and
the prophets who had constantly called the people to return to the
justice of God established in that law. When we read stories in the
New Testament about Jesus criticizing the law or when we read Paul
telling us that Christians are "free from" the law, we must be careful
to understand those remarks in the right spirit. Neither Jesus nor
Paul was against rules or against law as a necessary part of our social
life or even against the important part that the law had played in
forming the religious life of the Jewish people. Throughout the New
Testament, we find summaries of the decalogue and Old Testament
figures held up as examples of behavior that Christians should follow. Jesus and Paul are criticizing false views of the law which make
it a barrier to following God's will rather than a genuine revelation
of his love for his creation. Jesus criticizes certain accommodations
and interpretations of the law which set limits to "how far one has to
go" in loving obedience. These are examples of a false piety. He constantly refuses to join the Pharisees and make such legalistic interpretations, but that does not mean that he is rejecting the law as God
intended it [Schnackenburg, 1965:54]. Paul's struggle with the law is
somewhat different. He saw that through Jesus God was making sal-

vation available to all people, not just the Jews. But some Christians of Jewish descent did not agree. They thought that if non-Jews wanted to join the Christian movement, they would have to become Jews just like Jesus and the first disciples. This question plagued the early communities. Paul argued vigorously against the Jewish Christian view. Other apostles like Peter and Barnabas also agreed in principle, though they were willing to let churches hold a special "kosher" meal for Jewish Christians who did not want to eat with Gentiles, while Paul felt that this destroyed the unity that should be the basis of the community (read Acts 15 and Gal 2). Thus, Paul is critical of the law when it becomes a boundary to the universality of salvation. He is not critical of its ethical insight [Houlden, 1977:118; Stendahl, 1976:2–7].

The same attitude may be found in other ethical materials that Christians take over from their environment. Any ethical insight that is in harmony with God's will for his creation may be adopted by Christians. Jesus uses much proverbial wisdom in his teaching. Paul often quotes common Hellenistic ethical codes. For example, his praise of political authority in Rom 13:1–7 would be accepted by many people of his time as "what every reasonable person should think." But watch out for the context. Paul makes it clear that this Christian obedience is only because that order is God's, and it is also about to be subject to his judgment. Christians are not accepting the "divinity" which the emperor and his officials often claimed for the imperial order and its human embodiment. Jesus' own comment on the question of paying tribute to the Romans who held the Jews in captivity (Mk 12:13–17) has a similar ironic edge. He will not allow his opponents—who probably paid the tax themselves—to trap him into either taking an anti-Rome, revolutionary stand, "Don't pay," or granting the emperor the status he desired. The coin is Caesar's; it comes from his mint and bears his image. But neither it nor Caesar is God's [Schnackenburg, 1965:118]. These examples show how easy it is to miss the "critical edge" in what the New Testament is saying.

The question of eschatology and the ethical position of the New

Testament also has to take this "critical edge" into account. Jesus not only spoke of the closeness of God's rule, which many people thought would only be fully manifest at the judgment when evil was destroyed, he spoke of God's rule as something at hand, something people could come into contact with. The condition of seeing that God's rule is present and active in the world is a change of perspective. Instead of looking at the world as a place dominated by evil in which people have to struggle constantly to barely live up to the law, Jesus looks at the world as a place where good and evil are all mixed up, like the young plants in my garden. You can't pull up the weeds yet because if you try to do that you will destroy the baby plants (read Mt 13:24–30). Sometimes when the plants are very small, you can't even be sure which is which, so you wait and care for them both (read Mt 5:45). Jesus sees God caring for the world like that. There will be time to get the weeds, but, in the meantime, all sorts of good is also coming up, like those first radishes we had for supper tonight. Jesus sees this good breaking out when people are really able to look at others the way God does and not the way they think God ought to. One example of the way God looks at the world was based in the ministry of Jesus himself; he was open to sinners and outcasts, to anyone who wanted to approach him (including the Pharisees). This vision of God's nearness was the foundation of the behavior Jesus was showing his disciples. It was not a vision based on the impending threat of judgment. God's presence, then, forms the "critical edge" of much of Jesus' teaching. What is God's will in and for his creation? Act like that and you find the rule of God.

New Testament Ethics as a Call to Community

It is relatively easy for people who read the Bible to see that the whole biblical tradition insists that one's relationship to God is mirrored in one's ethical, not cultic, behavior. Ethics as the religious task is fundamental to the biblical experience of God [Schillebeeckx:587; Houlden, 1977:125]. But people today usually hear the word "ethics" as a reference to the behavior of the autonomous individual. They also often link ethics with the idea of a completely rational system of behavior, a universal code quite different from "irrational" commitments born of passion, preference, or community values. Frequently they think of ethics in terms of "duty," and as something unpleasant. Students in my freshman course on Western culture are quite convinced that virtue should be rewarded, at least in heaven, but they hardly know what to make of the classical idea that virtuous activity makes a person happy. And they have an equally difficult time with the biblical images of ethics as the response, or lack of it, of the community, which lives on the basis of its covenant relationship with God.

We cannot read the eschatological language of the New Testament correctly unless we remember that it is concerned with a new community which is being called into being. That community is the subject being addressed in the ethical advice of the New Testament. What is at stake is not the religious experience of private individuals, their triumphs and failures. What is at stake is a renewal of the community, the people of God. When the New Testament uses "perfectionist language" it is addressing the community as a place of holiness, not the isolated individual. This outlook has important consequences for the way in which Christians go about the task of ethics today. They must recognize their call to be an "all inclusive" gathering of God's people, a gathering that does not stop at personal, racial, sexual or national boundaries. Perhaps only such a community will be able to speak about the concerns that are facing all humans on the globe, not least the problem of what "human" should be "remade" by our ever-expanding technology [Jonas].

The New Testament Christians saw the presence of the Spirit at work in bringing this new community into being—even when individual members of the community were far from the ideals that it presented. Though they were able to draw upon the ethical traditions that surrounded them, they recognized the presence of the Spirit as a call not to be imbued with the values of the age in which they lived.

Their culture did not tell them what to value, whom to worship, whom to treat as neighbor. Such a direction could only come from God. Even though the final judgment did not come as soon as many of them expected, they saw, in the emergence of a new people of God based on the salvation brought in Jesus, the beginning and sign of the new age, which they expected to come with the judgment. Sometimes they would think that they had already attained all the fruits of salvation. Then Paul had to remind them that this new community still lives in hope. As a sign of God's presence, it also still lives in the imperfect world. The Christians never tried to isolate themselves to protect their perfection from the world any more than Jesus isolated himself. God's redemptive action is directed toward that world which is his creation [Houlden, 1977:123f].

The Style of Ethical Reflection

The remarks we have made so far already show that ethical reflection in the New Testament has a style which is different from the "tell me the rules to get the reward" model many people think of when they consider religious ethics. They want to know the rules they will have to play by and the "pay off" if they do. Then they think they can calculate. Either it's worth it or it's not. You may have already gathered that nothing could be further from the spirit of Jesus' teaching. He refused to play the game of "tell me the exact rules" with the Pharisees. Instead, he kept talking about what God intended his creation to be. For example, read the dispute about divorce in Mt 19:3–9. We do not need to go into the legal complexities involved in disputes over the grounds of divorce in Jesus' time. That's what the Pharisees want Jesus to do, of course. But he refuses. He goes back to Genesis and tells them that what God intended and created was a unity of husband and wife. How could humans destroy God's created unity? Of course, things don't work that way. People are divorced. Moses permits it, as the Pharisees remind Jesus. Notice

Jesus' answer carefully. He does not deny divorce, but he refuses to give it the same status as what God has created. Jesus is not interested in the kind of legal question that comes in when we begin to accommodate "hardness of heart." If husband and wife really become "one flesh," they would not be able to imagine divorce. But the "hard of heart" will not be able to have that experience. In short, Jesus is contrasting the way in which his disciples will feel with the way in which the "hard-hearted" feel. He is not setting up a system of divorce law. Many of his words are like these. They almost look like laws, but they only work for people who live out of a different consciousness than that of the Pharisees. The "radical fidelity" to God's intention in creation is destroyed when people try to turn those words into a system of law [Schillebeeckx:591–93].

This example illustrates important features of much of the ethical teaching of the Bible, particularly in its proverbs and wisdom traditions. It is not aimed at establishing universal rules and norms but at showing us what is really going on in human behavior. Jesus is showing the Pharisees "what is really going on" in their debates about divorce. Often, we can find more than one approach to a problem in the Bible. They show us the different angles from which we may consider a situation. This multiple-angle approach has been called by one scholar an "operating paradox." But there is something important we have to remember about the Bible's paradoxes, and that too is clear in Jesus' encounter with the Pharisees: the Bible knows all about "hardness of heart," but it never gives up on the "perfectibility of personhood under God" [Fisher:309–10].

Since the Bible does not intend to establish ethics as a question of laws, punishments and rewards, we must be careful to understand the difference between the "legal" view of evil and the religious one. The religious view has certain peculiarities, which would destroy a legal system [Schillebeeckx:593–600].

1. The religious seeks to offer a future to those who have failed or are weak. Paul's treatment of the weak conscience in the idol meat controversy reflects this "monism of grace" [see Chapter Six].

2. The "critical edge" of New Testament ethics and its eschatological conviction that the community is not yet perfect implies an
on-going self-criticism. The community is constantly reminded that
it is to embrace all humans as the people of God.

3. God, not ethical behavior simply, is the source of salvation.
Humans can never claim that they create salvation or, for that matter, that they create values, justice, righteousness.

4. Likewise, humans cannot stand as the final judges. The religious view of evil does not trivialize evil or the seriousness of sin, but
it knows that we are not in charge of taking care of it all by ourselves. Rather, there is one who is greater than evil, whose mercy can
overcome evil.

Finally, we have seen how closely the ethical vision of the New
Testament is tied to its vision of how God acts, how he views the
world [Houlden, 1977:18–20]. Sometimes Christians use "love" to
express the unifying vision of the whole of God's action as it is presented in both the teaching and the actions of Jesus and the New
Testament tradition generally [Schnackenburg, 1965:90–109]. But
we have to be careful not to reduce that symbolic and inclusive use of
"love" to our images of private individual emotions. It encompasses
many injunctions to "selflessness" and to sacrifice for the other person [Houlden, 1977:13f]. It makes Jesus' policy of "breaking boundaries" a permanent part of the Christian task. Christians must avoid
isolationism, sectarianism, closed dialogue that addresses only the
converted, only the people who agree with you. Christians have a re-
sponsibility to speak about what is good in such a way that it really is
addressed to all of God's creation. The Bible never speaks about
these realities in abstract terms. Such terms are too general. They
can apply to many religions. Instead, it insists on telling stories of
how God acts, of how people act. It confronts us with puzzles and
paradoxes sometimes. Most of all, it wants us to learn to imagine the
world that God saw when he looked down on his creation and pro-
nounced it good.

STUDY QUESTIONS

1. How does the New Testament view the ethical traditions of the Old Testament?

2. Why is Jesus critical of the law? Give an example of his criticism.

3. Why does Paul say that Christians are "free from the law"?

4. What is the "critical edge" in the divorce controversy (Mt 19: 3–9)?

5. Give two examples of "God's view of creation" in the teaching of Jesus. What common misconceptions about the world was Jesus trying to change?

6. How would you answer someone who thinks that ethics in the Bible is a game of rules and rewards/punishments?

7. What makes the religious approach to evil different from the legal one? Give two examples of the difference.

1
THE DOUBLE LOVE COMMANDMENT

Mt 22:34–40//Mk 12:28–34//Lk 10:25–29

Study the three versions of the love commandment. Notice the differences between them. Each version has been formulated to reflect the situation of the Christians for whom the evangelist writes. The relationships between the three versions are complex enough to suggest that there were several versions of this commandment in circulation among the early Christians.

Matthew 22	Mark 12	Luke 10
But when the Pharisees heard that he had silenced the Sadducees, they came together.	And one of the scribes came up and heard them disputing with one another, and seeing that he answered them well, asked him,	
And one of them, a lawyer, asked him a question, to test him.		And behold, a lawyer, stood up to put him to the test, saying,
Teacher, which is the great commandment in the law? And he said to him,	Which commandment is the first of all? Jesus answered,	Teacher, what shall I do to inherit eternal life? He said to him, What is written in the law? And he answered,
	The first is, Hear, O Israel, the Lord, our God, the Lord is one;	

You shall love the Lord your God with all your heart, and with all your soul, and with all your mind.

This is the first and great commandment.
And a second is like it, You shall love your neighbor as yourself. On these two commandments hang all the law and the prophets.

and you shall love the Lord your God with all your heart and with all your soul and with all your mind, and with all your strength.

The second is this, You shall love your neighbor as yourself.

There is no other commandment greater than these. The scribe said to him, You are right, Teacher; you have truly said that he is one, and there is no other but he; and to love him with all the heart, and with all the understanding, and all the strength, and to love one's neighbor as oneself, is much more than whole burnt offerings and sacrifices. And when Jesus saw that he answered wisely, he said to him, You are not far from the kingdom of God. And after that, no one dared to ask him any question.

You shall love the Lord your God with all your heart and with all your soul and with all your strength, and with all your mind;

and your neighbor as yourself.

And he said to him, You have answered right.

Do this and you shall live.

The Love Command in Palestinian Judaism

In order to see how this story would have sounded to Jesus' audience we need to consider other versions of the love commandment that are known to us from the time of Jesus. The distinction between Palestinian and Hellenistic Judaism that we use to divide our examples should not be considered a rigid one. There were Greek cities and Greek influence within Palestine just as much as there was Greek influence on Jews living outside Palestine. The question, rather, is one of orientation. Some traditions seem to have developed out of inner Jewish concerns; others seem to have sought to make Judaism more intelligible in the larger Hellenistic environment.

The "love of neighbor" command in Lev 19:18 was often used to reinforce the boundaries of the Jewish community. Inscriptions on Jewish tombstones identify "loving one's brother," that is, one's fellow Jew, as a virtue that merits reward. Rabbinic sources show a similar interpretation of the passage [Berger:130–33]. The command to love one's fellow Jew appears in stories of the final instructions of the patriarchs along with other commandments from the decalogue as an indication of the exemplary righteousness that the patriarch wants his children to exhibit:

> Noah began to lay upon his sons the ordinances and commandments and judgments that he knew, and he exhorted his sons to observe righteousness, to cover the shame of their flesh, to bless their creator, honor father and mother, love their neighbor, and guard their souls from fornication, uncleanness and all inquity.
>
> [Jub vii,20]

A more extended exhortation, given by Abraham, includes the love of neighbor and of God among a whole collection of commandments:

> And he commanded them that they should observe the way of the Lord; work righteousness; each love his neighbor,

and act in this manner among all men, each should walk with them so as to do righteousness and justice on the earth. . . . And guard yourselves from all fornication and uncleanness and pollution of sin, lest you make our name a curse. . . . I implore you, my sons, love the God of heaven and cleave to his commandments. Do not walk after their idols, and their uncleanness; do not make molten or graven gods, for they are vain, and there is no spirit in them; for they are the work of human hands and those who trust in them trust in nothing. Do not serve them or worship them but serve the Most High and worship Him continually.

[Jub xx,2–10]

This passage shows an extension of the commandment to the relations between Jews and the Gentiles among whom they live. The author wants to keep the community from being contaminated by the surrounding culture, especially its religious and sexual temptations. He also shows concern for the reputation which Jews might get. If they act with "love of neighbor" and justice toward all with whom they have dealings, then people will not reject them.

The commandment could also function in the opposite way. It could serve to define the boundaries of a particular group of Jews over against others. We find such a limitation among the Essenes. They tried to lead lives of strict obedience to the law following the interpretation of it handed on in their sect. They thought that most Jews had gone astray from the law and were destined for condemnation in the judgment. The "brother" whom a person is commanded to love is a fellow member of the sect:

Truly, they shall be careful to act according to the exact tenor of the Law in the age of wickedness and to separate themselves from the sons of the Pit, and to keep themselves from unclean riches of iniquity obtained with a vow or anathema, or by robbing the goods of the sanctuary, or by stealing from the poor of His people so as to make widows

of their prey. . . . To observe the Sabbath exactly as in the
Law, and the feasts and Day of Fasting according to the
commands of those who have entered the New Covenant in
the land of Damascus. To set holy things apart exactly as
in the Law. Each one to love his brother as himself, and to
support the needy, the poor and the stranger. Each one to
seek the well-being of his brother.

[CD vi,14–vii,2]

(For other examples of this use of "love of brother" see Berger:80–
103; 117–121.) The commandment of Lev 19:18 provides a key to relationships between members of the sect. The following passage interprets it as the foundation for rules about anger and revenge among
members of the sect:

And concerning what He said, "You shall take no revenge
and not bear malice against the sons of your people" (Lev
19:18): Anyone of the members of the Covenant who
brings an action against his fellow without having reproved
him before witnesses or brings an action in the heat of anger or tells the matter before his elders in order to dishonor
him is a man who "takes revenge and bears malice"; where-
as it is written that only "He takes revenge on his adversaries and bears malice against His enemies." (Nah 1:2)

[CD ix,2–5]

The prohibition against vengeance associated with the love command limits the kinds of legal action that are permitted between
members of the sect. Thus, it plays an important role in the strains of
everyday life.

From quite different positions in the community, both writings
are concerned with protecting the community. The Essenes wish to
protect their observance of the law in all its purity from the temptations to laxity and evil that they see around them. *Jubilees* hopes that

honorable conduct will win Jews good relations with their neighbors. However, contacts with outsiders must not lead people to adopt their customs, vain idolatry and immorality. Hence, love of the true God and the Jewish neighbor is to protect the community from those negative influences. Later, we will see the role that love commandments played in shaping the identity of the developing Christian community. Jesus himself did not seem to be concerned with either the legal aspects of the command or with defending the boundaries of Israel.

The Double Command in Hellenistic Judaism

The previous section provided examples of love of neighbor and love of God as part of the larger series of commandments. The move to summarize the commandments in the twofold love of God and neighbor appears in only two examples in Hellenistic Judaism [Berger:120;162f]. The double combination is usually expressed as "worship and fear of God" with "love of brother." An example of this combination can be found in *Jubilees.* The patriarch Isaac is instructing his sons Esau and Jacob:

> And I command you, my sons, that you practice righteousness and uprightness on earth so that the Lord will bring upon you everything he said he would do to Abraham and his seed. Love one another, my sons, your brothers as one loves his own self, and let each seek to benefit his brother. Act together on earth, and let each love the other as his own self. Concerning idols, I admonish you to reject and hate them. Do not love them, for they are full of deception for those who worship them and bow down to them. Remember, my sons, the Lord God of Abraham, your father, how I too worshipped Him and served Him in righteousness. Now I will make you swear a great oath . . . that you will fcar and worship him.
>
> [Jub xxxvi,3–7]

The story of Esau and Jacob was a natural place for reflection on the relationships between brothers. Another natural place for such reflection was the story of Joseph and his brothers. Examples of the double love command appear in the *Testaments of the Twelve Patriarchs,* an account of the last instructions of each of the patriarchs to his sons. (On the Hellenistic character of the Greek version of TestXII from which these examples come, see Harrelson:29f; Kee:262–70.) The following example seems to be the closest to the form of the double command in the tradition which Mark used [Berger:127f]:

> My children, keep the Law of God. Have singleness (of heart) and walk in guilelessness, not meddling in the business of your neighbor. But, love the Lord, and your neighbor; have compassion on the poor and the weak.
>
> [TIss v,1–2]

The patriarch Issachar goes on to hold himself up as an example. Some interpreters think that the love command here does not refer simply to one's fellow Jew but intends to refer to any person with whom one deals. You will also notice that this version adds the specification "with my whole heart" to love of neighbor rather than to love of God as we find it in the Gospel versions:

> Except my wife, I have not had any woman; nor have I committed fornication with my eyes. I was not led astray by drinking wine. I did not covet anything desirable that belonged to my neighbor. No guile arose in my heart. No lie passed my lips. If anyone was in distress, I joined my sighs with his, and I shared my bread with the poor. I was pious and kept truth my whole life. I loved the Lord, and also every man with my whole heart.
>
> [TIss vii,2–6]

Though these examples do not reduce the whole law to the double commandment, they do give that commandment a prominent place at the end of a list of commandments. That position presents it as what holds them all together. It concludes another such list in the following passage:

> Therefore, my children, observe the commandments of the Lord, and keep His Law. Depart from wrath. Hate lying, that the Lord may dwell among you and Beliar (=Satan) flee from you. Let each speak truthfully to his neighbor, so you will not fall into wrath and confusion but will live in peace, having the God of peace, so no war will prevail over you. Love the Lord all your life and one another with a true heart.
>
> [TDan v,1–3]

Our next example makes the double command proof against the temptations of Satan. It makes the patriarch Joseph the example of how the righteous person will stick by the law no matter what happens to him:

> My children, love the Lord God of heaven and earth, and keep his commandments, following the example of the good and holy man Joseph. Keep your mind on what is good, for the person whose mind is right sees everything correctly. Fear the Lord, and love your neighbor. Even though the spirits of Beliar claim you, to afflict you with every evil, they will not conquer you, just as they did not conquer Joseph, my brother. How many wanted to kill him, and God protected him! For, whoever fears God and loves his neighbor cannot be struck by Beliar, since he is protected by his fear of God. Nor can he be ruled by human artifice or by beasts, since he is helped by the Lord because of the love which he has for his neighbor.
>
> [TBenj iii,1–5]

Love of God and neighbor is the basis of the protection of the righteous person. Later in the same testament, we find an extensive description of the good person as one whose compassion and non-retaliation conquer evil:

> The good man does not have a dark eye, for he shows mercy to all, even though they are sinners. And, though they devise evil against him, he overcomes evil by doing good, since he is protected by God and loves righteousness as his own self. . . . He praises the virtuous; on the poor, he has mercy; on the weak, compassion, and to God, he sings praises. . . . If, then, you have a good mind, wicked men will be at peace with you, and the profligate will reverence you and turn to good, and the covetous will not only abandon their desire, they will give the objects of their covetousness to the afflicted. . . . If anyone does violence to a holy person, he repents because the holy person is merciful to his reviler and holds his peace. If anyone betrays a righteous person, the righteous one prays. Though he is humbled for a little while, yet, he will soon appear even more glorious as my brother Joseph did.
>
> [TBenj iv,1–v,5]

The Joseph examples extend the conduct of "love" and mercy beyond the relations between fellow Jews to any relationships in which the righteous person is involved. Love and compassion dictate one's behavior in the face of all affliction and enmity.

The Greek version of TestXII from which these examples come shows considerably more influence of common Hellenistic philosophy and language than the Synoptic sayings do. However, fragments of an Aramaic version of Testaments of Levi and Napthali are among the Essene writings found at Qumran. The presence of an Aramaic version there suggests that the traditions which underlie our present TestXII also circulated in other forms at the time of Jesus. Such stories and exhortations probably formed part of the general religious "wisdom" passed on among the people. Jesus could well have formulated his teaching in reference to such traditions.

"Love of Brother" and Hellenistic Friendship Ethics

"Love of brother" provided an important link between Jewish ethical traditions and those of the surrounding culture. Jews were often accused of "hatred of humanity" because they refused to assimilate to the larger culture, even under considerable pressure to do so such as we see reflected in *Jubilees*. They could use the "love of neighbor" tradition as an answer to such polemic. Usually, this apologetic is expressed in terms of the "mercy" or "compassion" which the righteous Jew shows to all [Berger:104–114; Fuller:48 on TIss vii,6]. Jews understood the Law as epitomizing the virtuous conduct intended for all humans. They summarized it using the Greek virtues of piety and friendship, which could easily be seen as love of God and neighbor. This interpretation provided Jews with a positive assessment of the Gentiles with whom they had to deal, an assessment that was necessary for their life in the larger community. The Gentile could be included in the category "friend" and might also be the object of missionary activity [Berger:123–62].

The legend of the translation of the Old Testament into Greek for the great library at Alexandria included exchanges between the Jewish translators and the Ptolemaic king. The answers of the translators proved the wisdom inherent in the Jewish tradition. The following section presents the Jewish law as the epitome of virtue:

> The king asked the sixth to answer the question, "To whom should we show gratitude?" He replied, "Continually to our parents, for God has given us a most important commandment on honoring parents. Next, He considers the attitude of friend toward friend, for He says, 'A friend is like your own self' (Dt 13:6). You do well in trying to bring all men into friendship with yourself." The king

spoke favorably to him and asked the next, "What is it that resembles beauty in value?" He said, "Piety, for it is the supreme form of beauty, and its power lies in love, which is the gift of God."

[Aristeas 228–229]

Piety, honor toward parents, friendship toward all provide the categories in which the injunctions of the Old Testament law can be translated into categories of virtue familiar to a Hellenistic audience. Another example of such translation comes from the first century A.D. Jewish philosopher, Philo of Alexandria. He provided Jewish readers with elaborate allegories of the law, which sought to show that the real teaching of the law was philosophic progress of the soul in virtue. Here are two examples in which the love of God and neighbor appear in Stoic categories of virtue [see Fuller:49f]:

But among the vast number of particular truths and principles there studied, two stand out high above the others as two heads: one, duty toward God as shown by piety and holiness; the other, duty toward men as shown by humanity and justice.

[Spec. Leg. ii,63]

For the nature which is pious is also kindly, and the same person will exhibit both qualities, holiness toward God and justice to men.

[Abr 208]

These Hellenistic Jewish traditions played an important role in early Christian ethical preaching, when the Christians found themselves engaged in preaching to the Gentiles. Luke seems to have made extensive use of the traditions of Hellenistic friendship ethics in his writings as a way of instructing Gentile converts in their ethical obligations as Christians. However, the New Testament never completely assimilates its message to such philosophical categories. The

New Testament writers do not think that Jesus was preaching an eternally valid philosophic wisdom. They present the message as an eschatological call to salvation.

The Double Command Tradition in the New Testament

This lengthy journey into the world of Jewish ethical teaching helps us appreciate the importance of such teaching about love of God and neighbor at the time of Jesus. Sometimes Christians have the false idea that Christianity invented love, mercy and compassion. Of course, the Gospel stories never claim to. All of them, in fact, play on the fact that the people who are questioning Jesus or trying to trap him really do know the answer to the question. The wisdom traditions of Judaism had been using friendship categories to understand love of neighbor [Berger:250f, who sees the culmination of this tradition in John; cf. Wis 6:18]. Jesus' preaching is not simply based on such wisdom traditions, however. It also has something in common with the Essenes, since, as we saw in the Introduction, he is calling into being a new community. His community (not the new covenant of the Essenes) represents the gathering of the righteous, of those who stand under the rule of God. Thus, the love command in Jesus' preaching combines wisdom and apocalyptic traditions [Fuller:51f]. The introductions to the Synoptic versions of the double command make it clear that the early Christians understood it as an answer to how one attained the salvation promised by Jesus. They did not understand it as a legal maxim or as a demonstration of the philosophic wisdom of Jesus.

Jesus' version of the love command has some features which we have not seen demonstrated in the parallel versions exactly. There is no formal parallel to the combination of the "one God" from Dt 6 and the "love neighbor" from Lev 19 that we find in Mk (so Berger:128, who considers TIss v,2 our closest parallel to Mk). Second, Jesus' version lacks any of the concern with the boundaries of the community so common in the other versions. Jesus seems to have sought to overcome boundaries which separated people. The positive evaluation of his teaching given by the scribe in the Markan version preserves that concern [so Piper:92–94].

Just as we have seen that there was no verbally identical teaching of the love of God and neighbor in the various Jewish examples, so there is no verbal identity in the Synoptic examples either. Nor is it possible to reduce them to a single version and argue that each evangelist has modified that version. Rather, just as can be seen to be the case in the Jewish examples, the importance of the commandment and its many applications seem to have generated different variations from the beginning. Some features common to the Mt/Lk version suggest a tradition independent of the one used by Mk. The introduction of a "lawyer," "one from" ("a certain" in Lk), seems to derive from a different tradition. The same tradition may have lacked the Shema (Dt 6:4), a feature which is presupposed by the subsequent elaboration of the command in Mk 12:32f [Berger:203; Fuller:44]. Mt 22:36 has "great" where Mk has "first." Mt 22:38 has combined both traditions [Fuller:45]. Similarly, Mt seems to have made a superficial change in Mk's introduction to the second commandment. He has probably used it where the tradition was similar to Lk without numerical introduction. We have no way of saying whether Mk introduced the numerical ordering at this point or whether it belonged to the version that Mk had received as tradition [Fuller:45]. The original qualification of the love of God clause was probably a triple "heart, soul, strength" as in Dt 6:5. The introduction of "mind" (or understanding)) probably represents Hellenistic influence as in TBenj iv,1–v,5. Mt's version seems to be derived from Mk [so Grundmann:477f]. Mk 12:30b itself may represent a conflation of two versions of the saying that were in circulation [so Berger:183].

Luke. If you look at the larger context of this passage in Lk, you will see that he is using this incident to serve as a frame for the parable of the Good Samaritan. He is not at all interested in the question of the Law and even changes the question so that it focuses on salvation in general. His entire section builds up to the application given in 10:37, "Go and do likewise." You will also notice that the lawyer, not Jesus, gives the double command. For Lk, that incident is still the preface to the discussion of salvation which culminates in the parable. Compare this section with the story of the rich young man in Lk 18:22–30. There, "giving alms" is added to the young man's reference to the decalogue as the key to salvation. Thus, the issue becomes one of going from the general ethical truths of the decalogue or, as here, the summary of the decalogue in the love commandments to discipleship. Jesus' parabolic definition of "neighbor" belongs to the Lucan teaching on what it means to be a disciple of Jesus. He has formulated that teaching in terms familiar to Hellenistic readers: the neighbor is one who shows "mercy." Hellenistic Jewish texts commonly use "mercy" for "love" in speaking about relations with the neighbor [Berger:232–42].

Matthew. In contrast to Lk, Mt is very much interested in the question of Jesus' relationship to the law. He has reformulated the tradition in 22:40 to make it clear that what is involved is the Christian principle of interpreting the law. Mt 7:12 gives another summary of the "law and the prophets," this time in the Golden Rule. The expression "hang" appears in the legal exegesis of the rabbis. Mt wants to make it clear that Christian interpretation of the law, based on Jesus' eschatological fulfillment of the law, is represented in the double commandment. It represents the foundation and intention of the whole law [Berger:207–31; Fuller:45; Grundmann:477f]. Mt's story is very short and to the point. This short formulation intensifies the sharpness of the break between Jesus and the tradition of Jewish teaching.

Mark. Mk's version of the story suggests that it had been used as part of the preaching to Gentiles. Look up 1 Thes 1:9f. It is a short formula from Paul's mission of preaching to Gentiles. You will notice that such preaching had to begin (which preaching to Jews did not) with teaching the worship of the one true God. We have already seen this concern for the true God as opposed to the pagan idols from the Jewish side in the *Jubilees* passage. When the story came to be used among Christians, who did not need such a reminder, simply as the key to righteousness, either in fulfillment of the law (so Mt) or in true virtue (so Lk), the stress on the first commandment would not have been as necessary. Indeed, most of the love commandments in the New Testament concern themselves simply with the love of neighbor.

You will also notice that without the last verse, the story in Mk is not hostile in tone. The scribe asks his question because Jesus is answering others well. The last verse suits Mk's context, since this story is part of a final collection of controversies between Jesus and his opponents. (Mt retains the location of the story in the narrative but has moved v 34 to follow the final story in the chain, one in which Jesus asks his opponents a question about the Son of David.) Thus, it stands as the final public answer Jesus gives about his teaching in Mk. (Lk has it much earlier in his account of Jesus' ministry.) For Mk it represents part of the final silencing of the Jews. However, the tradition that Mk received may have had a much more irenic tone. We shall see that Jesus himself tried to win the "scribes and Pharisees" over to his view of God's action.

There is a third feature of Mk's story, which was important in the Hellenistic mission. Remember, part of the mission to the Gentiles included the conviction that they did not have to become Jews in order to be saved. The lengthy speech which the scribe gives at the end of this story sets this commandment over against cultic obligations. Berger suggests that the story as it was used in the tradition of the Markan community represented the scribe as a seeker after wisdom (as in Wis 6:17–20). He comes to Jesus, the mediator of wisdom, and leaves with a new understanding of the law gained from that wisdom. Thus, the story explains how Christians can worship the true God and stand in the Old Testament tradition without continuing to follow the ritual and cultic obligations of the law.

Jesus. You can see from the different versions of the story that each evangelist has shaped the tradition so that the message of Jesus is applied to Christians in his day. You can also see that the tradition used by Mk had had considerable importance in missionary outreach to the Gentiles prior to its inclusion in his Gospel. You can also see that the differences in the versions suggest that several accounts of the double love command were in circulation among Christians. It would be foolish to suppose that we could somehow harmonize the three Synoptic versions and extract the exact wording of an incident in the life of Jesus. But that does not mean that the story tells us nothing about Jesus himself.

The combination of wisdom tradition and an apocalyptic summons to live in the light of the rule of God rather than according to detailed legal prescriptions coheres very well with the picture of Jesus' preaching that is preserved for us at various levels of tradition [Fuller:51f]. The elements of hostile controversy and rejection of Judaism in the story seem to come from the situation of the evangelists, when Christians were forced to defend their understanding of the law over against Judaism. The original story seems to have been much more irenic, a form of Scholastic debate. We can easily see Jesus drawing on a tradition of summarizing the law in the double love command to answer challenges about the intent of the law. Such traditions would fit very well with the tendency in the teaching of Jesus to appeal to God's intention in creation. Jesus could easily have used the double love command to point an audience toward "what is really at stake" in the revelation of the law. The various interpretations by early Christians and by the evangelists are ways of applying that teaching to their specific situations.

STUDY QUESTIONS

1. Note the differences in the three versions and then pick out those differences which each evangelist is using to apply the story to the specific situation of his audience.

2. Give an example of each of the following uses of the love of neighbor/brother within Judaism at the time of Jesus: (a) to mark the boundaries of the community; (b) to regulate relationships between members of the community; (c) to explain how Jews should relate to non-Jews; (d) to show how Jews should face hostility from outsiders; (e) to explain the value or truth of the Old Testament ethical tradition.

3. How does Lk use the double love command to present the key to salvation?

4. What is the relationship between the double love command and the law in Mt? In Mk?

5. Give two examples of how the Markan version of the story is suited to preaching to the Gentiles.

6. How does the double love command "fit in with" the general outlook presented in Jesus' teaching?

2
LOVE OF ENEMIES

Mt 5:43–48//Lk 6:27–28, 32–36

Study the two versions of the sayings on love of enemies. Pick out any of the special features of Mt or Lk that you also saw in each evangelist's version of the double love command.

Matthew 5:43–48	Luke 6:27–28, 32–36
You have heard that it was said, "You shall love your neighbor and hate your enemy," but I say to you, Love your enemies,	But I say to you that hear, Love your enemies, do good to those who hate you, bless those who curse you,
and pray for those who persecute you, so that you may be sons of your Father who is in heaven; for he makes his sun rise on the evil and on the good, and sends rain on the just and on the unjust.	pray for those who abuse you.
For if you love those who love you, what reward have you? Do not even the tax-collectors do the same?	If you love those who love you, what credit is that to you? For even sinners love those who love them.

27

And if you salute only your brethren what more are you doing than others?
Do not even the Gentiles do the same?

And if you lend to those from whom you hope to receive, what credit is that to you?
Even sinners lend to sinners, to receive as much again.
But love your enemies,
and do good,
and lend, expecting nothing in return;
and your reward will be great,
and you will be sons of the Most High;
for he is kind to the ungrateful and selfish.

You, therefore, must be perfect, as your heavenly Father is perfect.

Be merciful, even as your Father is merciful.

Love of Enemy, Non-Retaliation and Divine Judgment

Sometimes love of enemy is understood as non-retaliation. In such examples, it serves to regulate relationships between members of a community, just as love of brother does, and to insure that feuds and vengeance do not destroy the community. We have already seen examples of Jewish traditions about the need to surmount hostility between brothers—Esau and Jacob or Joseph and his brothers. Jewish wisdom traditions contain warnings about the destructive character of anger and vengeance (see Prov 25:21f; Sir 27:30–38:7). Apocalyptic preaching, like that among the Essenes, could moderate demands for vengeance now in the expectation that God would avenge the community against its enemies at the judgment. The sectary might even be said to have added to the condemnation that will come upon his enemy because he did not retaliate [so Stendahl,

1962]. Thus, the Essene is instructed to do good and leave all judgment to God:

> I will not render the reward of evil to anyone. I will pursue each one with goodness, for the judgment of all the living belongs to God, and He is the one who will pay each his reward. I will not envy from a spirit of wickedness. My soul will not covet the riches gained from violence. As for the multitude of men of the Pit, I will not lay hands on them until the Day of Vengeance, but I will not withdraw my anger from perverse men. I will not be content until He begins the Day of Judgment.
>
> [1 QS x,17–20]

Though the sectary does not try to avenge himself on the evil, he still hates wickedness. This teaching not only instructs him not to take vengeance but to leave judgment to God, but it also serves an important emotional function. It instructs him not to envy those whose violence and disregard for the law seem to be gaining them riches.

The certainty of divine vengeance and judgment can also make people willing to endure evil as in the following passages:

> I have written down everyone's work. No one born on earth can remain hidden or his works be concealed. I see all things. Now, my children, spend your days in patience and meekness, that you may inherit eternal life. Endure every wound, every injury, every evil and attack for the Lord's sake. Do not return evils either to a neighbor or an enemy because the Lord will return them for you and be your avenger on the Day of Great Judgment, that there be no vengeance here among men.
>
> [II Enoch 1,1–4]

Bear every painful and cruel yoke that comes upon you for
the Lord's sake, and thus you will find your reward in the
Day of Judgment.

[II Enoch 1i,3]

Both these traditions mitigate the actual and emotional effects of
vengeance in human communities. Individuals are not to be consumed with envy at what might appear to be the good fortune of
those who choose to neglect the law. They are not to assume that
such people actually "get away with it." However, the love which is
being extended to such people seems to be limited in scope. The enemy against whom one does not retaliate is still the object of hatred
and divine vengeance.

   Now look at the Gospel passages. You can see something of the
"critical difference" in this teaching. There is nothing about God's
vengeance here—not even "I won't retaliate but I will hate evil." Instead, there are two types of argument, both close to wisdom traditions in style. The first: There is nothing so special about hating
enemies and loving friends. Anyone—tax-collector, Gentile, sinner—
does that. The second: God doesn't behave that way. Mt gives a nature analogy to explain the inclusive character of God's action. Lk's
reasoning is in a simple statement: God is kind to just and unjust.
Both insist that the reason for non-retaliation is a likeness to God. If
you looked closely at the two versions, perhaps you also noticed
something else about their choices of examples for "sinners." Mt has
used a typically Jewish combination for the despised outsiders, "tax-
collectors and sinners." This passage can then remind the Jewish
Christians in his audience that they can and should go out to the
Gentiles. Lk, on the other hand, is concerned with the problem of
wealth. His specific example is lending money. It ties in with his concern to instruct wealthy Gentile converts in the obligations of Christian charity.

Non-Retaliation and Love of Enemy as Sign of Philosophic Virtue

We have seen that Hellenistic ethical reflection played an important role in the interpretation of the "love of neighbor" commandment among Jews who sought to explain the philosophic truth of their understanding of virtue. We find a similar situation when we turn to love of enemies. Cynic/Stoic philosophers of the time viewed non-retaliation and love of enemy as a sign of the philosopher's freedom from and superiority to the passions and illusions of the masses. A person not caught up in those passions cannot be injured. Similarly, the gods are not injured by the ungrateful behavior of the humans on whom they bestow benefits [Piper:20f]:

> If you are imitating the gods, you say, "Then bestow benefits also upon the ungrateful; for the sun rises also upon the wicked, and the sea lies open to pirates." This point raises the question whether a good man would bestow a benefit on an ungrateful person if he knew that he was ungrateful. Understand that according to Stoicism there are two classes of ingrate: one type is ungrateful because he is a fool; another—the common meaning of the term—because he has a natural tendency to this vice. The good man will benefit the first type of ingrate, but he will no more benefit the second type than he would lend money to a spendthrift or to a person whom many have already found to be false.
>
> [Seneca, De Beneficiis iv,26]

Thus, Seneca does not exactly tell the Stoic to imitate the gods, since he makes distinctions about the character of the person in question. However, the wise person never reacts to injury with anger, vengeance or any other such passion, since he has conquered the passions. It would be unworthy of the philosopher, who is superior to the masses, to take vengeance on an inferior [cf. Seneca, De Ira ii 32,1f,iii 42,3.4; 43,1.2; De Constantia iv,1].

Hellenistic Jewish writings also use this Stoic vision of superior tranquility as the basis for non-retaliation. Aristeas states that Judaism is superior to pagan philosophy because it combines philosophical freedom from passion with devotion to God (235) and that God assists people in achieving this philosophic ideal:

> The king asked another, "What is philosophy?" He explained, "To deliberate well concerning any question that arises; and never to be carried away by impulses, but to reflect on the injuries that result from passions; and to act rightly in all circumstances, practicing moderation. But we must pray to God to instill a regard for these things into our mind."
>
> [Aristeas 256]

The "benefit" which such a person shows in the face of injury may have the added advantage of turning the evil person toward the good:

> The king asked the next, "To whom should one show liberality?" He replied, "All agree that we ought to show liberality toward those who are well disposed toward us, but I think that we ought to show the same spirit of generosity toward those who are opposed to us so that in this way we may win them over to what is right and to what is advantageous to us. But we must pray to God that this be accomplished, for He rules the minds of all."
>
> [Aristeas 227]

Philo also argues that love benefits the person who acts with generosity toward an enemy and that that generosity toward an enemy may even end the feud between the two parties (Virt 116–118). These examples show that non-retaliation or generosity toward an enemy can be seen as a sign of superior virtue. The philosopher is the author of his own virtue. The Jew, on the other hand, argues that God assists people to achieve these goals because He is the one who controls the minds of humans, not the unaided reason.

Love of Enemy in the Joseph Traditions

The Joseph tradition developed its own variations on the theme of love of enemy in telling the story of Joseph and his brothers. God is shown to be the one who rescues a person who does not retaliate but does good to his enemy [cf. Harrelson; Hollander]:

> If you, therefore, walk in the commandments of the Lord, my children, He will exalt you and bless you with good things forever. And if anyone seeks to do evil to you, do good to him and pray for him and the Lord will rescue you from all evil.
>
> [TJos xviii,1–2]

Joseph and Asenath, a romance of Joseph's marriage to the daughter of an Egyptian priest after her miraculous conversion to Judaism, concludes with a plot against Joseph hatched by Pharaoh's son, who had wanted to marry the beautiful girl. He draws some of Joseph's brothers into the scheme. The principle that a pious person does not "return evil for evil" occurs several times. First, Levi uses it to keep Simeon from killing Pharaoh's son for proposing such a scheme to them (23,9); next, Asenath in explaining why she is willing to plead for the brothers who had tried to abduct her, states that the pious person does not "render evil for evil to any person" (28,4); again, Asenath offers the added comment that the Lord will provide revenge for the outrage (28,14); finally, Levi tells Benjamin that he should not have struck Pharaoh's son. The pious person does not "render evil for evil or stamp on one who has fallen, or torture the enemy to death." Rather, one should cure the enemy from his wound and "if he lives, he will be your friend, and his father, the Pharaoh, will be your friend"(29,3–4). This tale applies the principles of love

of enemy to the tensions experienced by Jews living in Egypt, especially those caused by intermarriage with the pagan population and
the Jewish desire (requirement?) that the pagan spouse convert.

The principle of non-retaliation applies to a specific situation of
conflict which the Jew hopes to ameliorate by not retaliating for any
injury that he/she might suffer. Another example of such motivation
is given in Josephus. He suggests that "love of enemy" will not only
demonstrate that the charges of "hatred of the human race" often
launched against the Jews are false but it may also lead the hostile
party to become a proselyte [Contra Apion ii,209–17]. The motivation of conversion of the enemy is much more frequent in Jewish
sources than in Stoic ones. Compare JosAsen 29,4: the enemy may
be converted into a friend. The Stoic tradition sees the enemy's action as proof that he has no rational self-control. The Jewish concern
about the effect of non-retaliation on the attitude of the enemy reflects the problems of a minority community that is trying to survive
in surroundings that are suspicious and sometimes openly hostile.

This concern with the effect of one's behavior on hostile and
suspicious adversaries will also appear in some of the New Testament teachings on love as we shall see. Some of the elements of the
Cynic/Stoic teaching on love of enemies are reflected in the Lucan
passage. Perhaps they had become proverbial examples.

Love of Enemies When the Parties Are Unequal

One might look at the Jewish and Christian concern with the
effect of non-retaliation on a suspicious public as nothing more than
pragmatic "good sense." They had no real alternative. The philosophic tradition reflected in Seneca also takes the question of the relative status of the parties involved into account. We have already
seen that the non-retaliation of the philosopher demonstrates his superiority to the person who offends him. The philosophers consider
two other cases of inequality. First, a slave or other person dependent upon someone more powerful must exercise self-control when

abused rather than attempt to retaliate. Such behavior represents the Stoic view that the wise person will always adapt to those circumstances beyond his/her control. Second, at the other end of the spectrum, a victorious king will forego vengeance against his enemy. By showing the enemy unexpected mercy the king may convert the enemy into a friend (cp. JosAsen 29,4; in the story the Pharaoh's son dies and Joseph gains the throne of Egypt, a legend reflected in Josephus' *Antiquities* ii, 174; Wis 10:14; TLevi xiii,9). The latter is hardly relevant to early Christians. They will, however, adopt some of the pragmatic advice of the Hellenistic ethical tradition in advising slaves on their behavior [see Schottroff:17–20].

The various examples of love of enemy show a considerable range. Perhaps the first thing to notice is that the command has no concern or interest in positive inner emotions toward such a person. The only extended concern with emotion appears in connection with the rejection of envy that the righteous might feel at the prosperity of the wicked. Nor does love of enemy necessarily involve any desire that that enemy not experience the punishment that is rightfully due his/her offense. The question is always whether, and to what extent, individuals might become involved in retaliation. These teachings suggest that there are situations in which the tendency toward retaliation is better deferred. The motivations for such behavior are often tied to the social status of those involved. The philosopher demonstrates his superior conquest of passion. A minority group hopes to allay the suspicions of a hostile public. A small, close-knit sect cannot afford the destructive consequences of revenge or the emotional toll of envy. The slave simply hopes to survive. Or, perhaps, a benefit will derive from the unexpected conversion of the enemy into a friend. These examples also make it clear that actual situations of injury were envisaged when people talked about "love of enemy." Even the king, who can afford to be generous because he has won, nevertheless suffered the distress of having to fight a war. It would make very little sense to talk about love of enemy to those who do not have the experience of being the "injured party."

Love of Enemies in the Synoptic Tradition

Understanding the various contexts in which love of enemies was discussed helps us to locate the New Testament discussions within that spectrum of opinion. The versions of the command that we have in the Synoptic tradition involve a more radical renunciation of vengeance than we find in those traditions which promise that God will take up where we leave off. At the same time, they are not aimed at the general philosophic conquest of passion. Rather, they are attached to the image of God which is part of the presence of the rule of God proclaimed by and exemplified in Jesus [Meier:260–64; Piper:56]. The examples also support those exegetes who insist that when Jesus gave this teaching he had specific hatreds and tensions within the community in view [so Grundmann:177]. Other examples of love commands in the New Testament specify the types of injury involved along with the response as we shall see. Lk may have generalized the saying by including the advice on lending to suit his concerns with the proper way for rich Christians to use their money [Johnson; Karris]. They are constantly enjoined to give freely rather than to follow the common Hellenistic pattern of generosity to equals and peers (sinners expect to get back what they give). But in making that combination, Lk is also following traditions known to his audience, since the Seneca example showed that lending was part of the discussion over "divine benefits." Mt's "salute your brethren/the Gentiles do the same" may stem from social problems in his community. Mt seems to have been written for a Jewish Christian community, which was turning outward toward the Gentiles as a result of the Pharisaic consolidation after A.D. 70. That consolidation seems to have been making the conversion of Jews more difficult. Mt himself favors this new direction [cf. S. Brown]. Both the initial focus on persecution and the encouragement to "salute others besides one's brethren" could well have been addressed to this situation.

The context of the saying in the SynTrad makes the parallel

with divine action primary rather than secondary as it is in the Stoic example. The shift of focus reminds us that the tradition does not stem from such general discussions of virtue. Rather, the basis for human action is how God treats "his enemies" in contrast with the way in which Jesus' contemporaries looked at questions of divine judgment and vengeance. Apocalyptic traditions like those in the Essene writings considered the present time as one of divine patience and mercy. It was rapidly drawing to a close and would soon be followed by God's judgment. We have seen that divine judgment was sometimes given as a motive for non-retaliation. People should use the present time of mercy to repent and be saved from the coming judgment. Those who fail to do so will be condemned:

> Until this day lasted the day of His mercy. He has been merciful and long-suffering toward those who dwell on earth. And when the Day, the power, and punishment and judgment come, which the Lord of Spirits has prepared for those who do not worship the righteous Law and who deny the righteous judgment and who take His name in vain— that Day is prepared: for the elect, a covenant; for the sinners, an inquisition.
>
> [I En 1x,6–8]

Another apocalyptic writing, II Baruch, has the revealing angel show the seer the judgment and salvation that are coming. The angel is said to show him

> ... the suppression of anger, and the magnitude of long-suffering, and the truth of judgment, and the root of wisdom, and the riches of understanding, and the fount of knowledge. And the height of the air; the greatness of Paradise; the consummation of the ages, and the beginning of the Day of Judgment.
>
> [II Bar 1ix,6–8]

These apocalyptic traditions teach the righteous that God is being merciful and long-suffering in suppressing his anger at the wicked. At the same time, they teach the righteous that judgment is certainly on the way, a judgment which will vindicate their faithfulness just as it gives the evil what they deserve.

The tone of Jesus' saying is quite different. Divine patience with the wicked now appears in the analogy of sun and rain—probably derived from Jewish wisdom traditions. Its proverbial character may account for what appears to be a related proverb about sun, rain, the sea, and pirates in the Seneca passage. Rather than assure the audience that divine patience is about to end, the Synoptic saying presents the "patience of God" as a divine perfection. A perfection that humans might seek to imitate rather than to end. Thus, this divine attitude need not raise questions about the fate of evil in the world. Instead, it becomes in Jesus' teaching a sign of the presence of the rule of God, which is to reform and renew the ethical perceptions of humanity.

The Tradition of the Love of Enemy Saying

Once again, the differences between the versions of this tradition make it impossible to claim that either Mt or Lk represents an older tradition. Each may have had different oral or written traditions [Grundmann:175: perhaps all the Matthean antitheses were derived from a tradition of Christian exegesis of Lev 19:18]. The antithetical introduction to Mt's version seems to have been the work of the evangelist to fit this tradition in with others in the section. Thus, there is no need to try to discover a particular injunction to "hate enemies" in the "hate wickedness" of the psalms [Meier:247; on the Matthean introduction see Suggs].

Mt 5:44//Lk 6:27. Mt may have shortened a longer tradition when he created the antithetical form. The Lucan introduction fits a situation in which Christians were not facing any specific persecution. Rather, they are simply subject to sporadic hostility from non-Christian neighbors. We have seen that the combination "If anyone does evil to you, do good to, pray for him and the Lord will deliver you" occurs in TJos. Perhaps Lk knows a tradition which has the "do good and pray" sequence. A variant tradition in 1 Cor 4:12, which has been adapted to the situation of traveling Christian missionaries, has a threefold response: reviled—bless, persecuted—endure, and slandered—try to conciliate. Lk's curse—bless section may derive from such a missionary tradition, while the persecute—pray of Mt suggests the situation of Christians in settled communities rather than the wandering life of an apostle.

Mt 5:45//Lk 6:35. Since the TJos parallel concludes with a reference to God's action, perhaps some reference to the relationship between the person who loves the enemy and God is traditional in such sayings [Schurmann,346, thinks that Lk's tradition may have already separated the command from the comment on likeness to God]. Lk's ethical reformulation suits the Hellenistic philosophical preaching reflected in Seneca. Since Mt's formulation reflects liturgical usage with its "your heavenly Father," Lk 6:35c may preserve the traditional wording. These observations suggest that a saying of the form: *Love your enemies; do good to those who do evil to you, pray for those who curse you, that you may be sons of the Most High (or the Father?)* circulated as the early Christian love of enemies command.

Mt 5:46–47//Lk 6:32–34. We have already seen that the series of rhetorical questions which seek to add weight to and apply the saying itself bear the marks of the situations out of which each evangelist comes. The expression "tax-collectors" and "Gentiles" is typically Matthean [Walker:224–27]. The less derogatory remarks about sinners in Lk also seem to be the evangelist's work [Walker:227–29].

However, Mt's version has a nature analogy, which is more characteristic of the use of wisdom traditions in Jesus' preaching than it is of later Christian elaborations. Therefore, the saying probably had such an expansion from the beginning [Piper:60]. That expansion with the description of God's perfection would have served as the original motivation for such behavior.

Mt 5:48//Lk 6:36. Mt uses v 48 as the thematic summary for the whole section of the Sermon on the Mount. Lev 19:11 has the injunction: "Be holy as the Lord your God is holy." Dt 18:13 provides a parallel: "Be perfect before the Lord your God." Concern for perfection is typical of the community language of the Essenes. They are the "perfect of way" or "the perfect." Their community is the "house of perfection and truth in Israel to establish the covenant according to everlasting precepts" (1 QS xi,11,17). Thus, Mt's language in v 48 suggests that Christians are the ones who possess the holiness appropriate to the community of the new covenant [Grundmann:179–81]. Lk's formulation in terms of "mercy" is typical of Hellenistic Judaism and of New Testament paraenesis whenever its injunctions are not dependent upon the love command [Berger:127; 253–55]. The saying about being perfect/merciful parallels that about being sons of the Most High. It does not add anything to the latter, but the Matthean language about perfection does suggest that this Christian interpretation of the Torah, not the strict observance of Jewish sects like the Essenes or the interpretations of the Pharisees, is the foundation for the messianic community, the new covenant.

Since discussion about love of enemies always assumes that the person addressed has some reason to retaliate against an enemy, it would appear that Jesus' saying also had some of the enmities faced by his audience in view. The evangelists, quite properly, have shifted the application of the saying to make sure that their audience understands that it also applies to them. But Jesus also differs from what was commonly said and felt. We are not encouraged to await God's vengeance. We are not warned against envying sinners. Divine patience does not appear as a liability at all. Instead, the present perfection of divine patience and mercy is to motivate the required love of enemies. The community which embodies this perfection is the community of the new age.

STUDY QUESTIONS

1. Give two reasons why Jewish apocalyptic traditions exhort people not to take vengeance on their enemies.

2. Give two reasons why a Stoic philosopher would not seek vengeance against someone who had injured him.

3. Give two examples of non-retaliation from the Joseph tradition.

4. How does the love of enemies tradition in the New Testament differ from that in the philosophers? From that in Jewish apocalyptic writings?

5. Explain how each of the evangelists has applied the teaching on love of enemies to the situation of Christians in his community.

6. What does Jesus' teaching about love of enemies tell us about God?

3
METAPHORS ENABLING LOVE

God and the Difference It Makes

We have seen that the "critical difference" in much of Jesus' teaching can be tied to his way of envisioning God and his relation to creation. The love of enemies command, for example, uses a sharp pointed comparison from the wisdom tradition to indicate that such love belongs to the nature of God. Not only does it prove his perfection, it also represents the perfection of the new community that he calls into existence. Such a connection between human action and the nature of God is a common enough feature of the biblical tradition. Ethics is bound to a particular vision of God's activity and his intentions for humanity and the world. Thus, the biblical tradition never seeks to present its ethical demands as simply a system of rewards and punishments. Behavior springs from the way in which the community views itself in relation to God and God's creation.

Yet, the connection between ethics and the biblical vision of God is not as obvious in the twentieth century as it might have been in the first. Many people find it hard to make sense of the biblical view of God's activity in creation and history in light of the very different understanding of creation and history that is typical of our time. They think that perhaps they can retain a hold on biblical faith by simply continuing its ethical insights. Frequently, people attempt to present Jesus' teaching about love as a universal ethic which is quite independent of the images and convictions about God associated with it [Piper:69–75].

Neo-Marxist, political interpretations of Jesus sometimes present him as the opponent of a false religious consciousness. That false consciousness was embodied in the utopian predictions of Jewish apocalyptic speculation. It taught the righteous to be content with their suffering and oppression in this world because God would soon intervene to right all wrongs. Jesus, on the other hand, challenged the apocalyptic view. He presented the future as something that is solidly in the hands of humanity. He did not agree that human nature was fixed and unalterably evil but taught that humans could change themselves through their actions. The love command, then, becomes the cornerstone of Jesus' call for a liberated humanity [Machovec]. This interpretation catches some facets of Jesus' preaching rather well. He certainly was no pessimist or fatalist. He certainly did oppose some of the views of God and humanity implicit in the metaphorical language of apocalyptic as we have already seen. But one must ask whether his call to humanity would make any sense at all without a vision of the enabling presence of God. Further, that presence also implies a certain mystery about human moral action and liberation. It does not stem from a deliberate program, plotted and executed by human visionaries. Even the best human programs have a way of falling into "hard-heartedness" as Jesus' controversy over the proper understanding of the law shows. Today, some people would also point to the tremendous cost and suffering involved in attempts at humanly instituted programs of liberation. They ask whether there can be any real, consistent claims for human rights and equality without religious sponsorship, without the conviction that these tasks are mandated by God [Küng:662].

More common among biblical theologians is the suggestion that the "mythical" world-view of the first century, especially of Jewish apocalyptic, be reinterpreted using the categories of existential philosophy. We could then show what the Bible message should mean for people today apart from the unfamiliar world-view in which it is cast. What the interpreter has to do is to catch the implications for how humans should experience themselves and their world resident in the biblical language. The preaching of Jesus presents the experience of God's rule breaking into human life in terms of love. What that means in concrete terms has to be found in the urgency with which that love is tied to the neighbor. All of·the ultimacy and seriousness which people attach to the symbol "God" is made present when one makes a decision about how one relates to, loves or does not love, the neighbor [Bultmann:19–22]. Again, this view catches something important about the way in which Jesus has tied "God" and ethics together. But the translation into philosophical ethics misses the significance of the concrete turn one finds in the imagery of the biblical tradition. An appeal for human action through compelling images and stories is different from such an appeal in abstract categories. The metaphor and story have a way of capturing the imagination, of getting us to see ourselves and the world differently that is not really duplicated when the story is reduced to universal statements.

Finally, there are legions of psychological approaches to Jesus' language about the rule of God. They see it as concerned with a reorientation of the human psyche [see Niederwimmer from a Jungian perspective; Moore from a more eclectic psychological theory]. Certain dynamics of the human psyche construct and thrive on legalism. Love undermines them. In order to do so, it must unmask the real guilt that corrupts the human situation, our sense of failure before the transcendent. Jesus exemplifies the person whose relationships with God, self, and others are not corrupted by guilt and its projections [Moore]. Jesus lives from the Self, from his union with the transcendent, and not from the limited, defensive posturings of the human ego [Niederwimmer]. This approach, too, plays a valuable role in challenging us to imagine what living out of a consciousness of the rule of God might be like. It reminds us that we must be careful not to project our own psychic distortions onto Jesus.

However, many questions can be raised from the biblical side. The model identifies religious conversion with psychological integration as salvation. It suggests that the true Christian achieves Jesus' consciousness of self. While that may be a desirable goal, the New Testament authors faced and rejected first century variants of such claims. Consider the debate with the Stoics over the basis of love of enemy. For the philosopher, the soul must achieve a state free from the warring passions that dominate other humans. Both the Jewish and Christian traditions rejected that approach on the grounds that God is the one who controls the heart and mind of humans to make such love possible. Theologically, many people would object to any psychological interpretation that would reduce Jesus to being the exemplar of the transformed psyche, a model to be internally achieved by the believer, if it deprived Jesus of his unique place as mediator of salvation, of a new relationship between humanity and the divine. Finally, the psychological approach has the weakness of catering to the "self-absorption" of twentieth century Northern Europeans and Americans. Not only is such language inappropriate to the experiences of the rest of the world, it bypasses the language of human communities, their tensions and their solidarity before God that is a fundamental presupposition of biblical ethics.

In sum, "writing out God" means claiming that the truth of the biblical message is really a truth about some other subject: political liberation, philosophical ethics, depth psychology. The biblical message may, indeed, be significant for our reflection on all these areas, but it resists being reduced to them. God, it insists, acts and illuminates our human life, concerns and obligations from a perspective beyond human wisdoms. For his disciples, Jesus himself enabled realization of the presence of God's rule [Piper:76–81].

Preserving the Metaphor

The various strategies of interpretation we surveyed carried the advantage of turning from unfamiliar biblical language to language we read and hear elsewhere in our world. Yet they seem to have lost something in doing so. We recognize that the religious language of Jesus' time and the issues about which they were speaking when they used that language are not familiar to most people. We use extensive quotations from other writings of the time in order to overcome this unfamiliarity.

Another common mistake is to treat the metaphorical and symbolic passages of the Bible as though they were statements of fact. That mistake makes the "world" of Jewish apocalyptic, for example, much more bizarre, like a "Star Wars" film taken literally, than it need have been [Caird:183–271]. We have also seen that "mere words" are not everything we need to consider about language. We also need to consider the ways in which language functions. Remember the number of functions that the command "Love your neighbor" performed! The general functions of language can be divided into three types [Caird:1–36].

1. Referential. These are the kind of statements we make when we talk about people and things, or when we wish to convey information. It also embraces the processes by which we think, create and compare general concepts. When we talk about God, who is not an object in this world like the other things about which we talk, our ability to compare and form new concepts is all important. We cannot talk about God at all without using metaphors.

2. Commissive. These are the kind of statements we use to get things done. Commands are a form of this type of language. They carry a validity even if people do not obey them, though commands which are never obeyed may seem to be insignificant. Another form of language that we use in this way is emotive language, the language in which we express our feelings, our commitments, our values. Slogans and symbols often form an important part of such language.

3. Cohesive. These are the kind of statements we make that identify us as members of a particular social group, as "brothers" and "friends" rather than as enemies, as those who belong rather than as outsiders. Slogans and symbols also have their role to play here. So do dialect, slang, and maybe even special language such as that we use in speaking to small children. Merely dividing the human world into Jew/Gentile in the first century would mark a person as

Jewish. Similarly, Catholics tend to use Catholic/Protestant to divide the religious world in a way that Protestants rarely do. If you look back at the rhetorical questions Mt and Lk formulate for the love of enemies command, you can see little hints of the in-group/out-group language of their respective communities.

When we speak about love "commands," we place the love language in the New Testament in the second type of speech. It expects to get something done. We have seen that that "something" has very concrete dimensions when it is applied to non-retaliation in specific social settings. But we have also seen that it presupposes the other uses of language as well. Metaphorical statements about God are an important part of the context of that command. Other expressions like "sons of the Most High" are cohesive. The idea is that we want to belong to that group, and if we value such belonging, we will act as suggested. Much of the language of judgment in the Old Testament prophets and in Jewish apocalyptic has this cohesive function in view. We have already seen that "Defer vengeance to God" aims to make it possible for the community of the righteous to stay together despite the destructive emotions of anger between members or envy of outsiders free from the restrictions of that community. Comments like "Even the Gentiles do that" in Mt 5:46f trade on Jewish feelings of moral superiority to their Gentile neighbors to get them to adopt the teaching about love of neighbor. We use a similar tactic when we tell a child: "Don't act like a baby." We are trading on the child's growing sense of independence and possible adulthood to inspire him/her to adopt certain behavior.

Since religious language is inseparable from metaphor, the use of metaphor cannot be eliminated. However, it makes a great deal of difference to the tone and significance of a particular statement what metaphors are involved. The associations they carry may significantly change our response. We have already seen that Jesus' teachings on the love command shy away from metaphors of apocalyptic judgment in favor of creation-centered proverbial statements. Use of that type of speech changes the "feeling" about God and even the command itself that is generated by the metaphor. Proverbial language represents astute observation about the actual situations in which humans find themselves. One accepts or rejects the truth of a particular proverb on the basis of a certain "recognition" of its appropriateness to the human situation—even if that recognition is cast in a metaphor that is more exaggerated or comic than those we ordinarily would use to describe human behavior. Judgment language, on the other hand, usually motivates either through fear of the consequences or expectation of the reward for certain behavior. Since experiences of such divine judgment are not part of the ordinary human world, the descriptions of them have to appear in metaphors of grandeur, even fantastic and elaborate detail. Such "monumental" speech aims to persuade us of the seriousness of what is at stake in the judgment.

The contrast in scale between the grand and fantastic judgment and the illuminating, everyday languages of proverbial traditions provides an important clue as to how God's presence works. Jesus uses the wisdom language with its appeals to nature and human experience to point to the divine presence as something that is around, at hand, part of our world. At the same time, those metaphors of divine presence surround rather extraordinary suggestions about humans and their behavior. That is not something that is taken for granted at all. Nor does Jesus ever follow the "That's the way human folly is" attitude of the wisdom traditions. Mt has caught the special, revolutionary experience of this presence of God and the surprise inherent in Jesus' exhortations by framing the love of enemies command as part of a series of antitheses. Customary human behavior is one thing. Jesus' is quite another.

Parables as Enabling Stories

Jesus also uses more extended metaphors to convey his sense of the new possibilities of human action that are opened up by the presence of the kingdom, the parables. Two of them, which are miniature stories, will be the topic of the next two chapters. Jesus' parables are a mixture of realism and exaggeration. A non-metaphorical conscious-ness tends to turn them into allegories to make a single point and therefore misses the dynamics of what is meant to happen to the per-son who hears these stories. The parables show us the kinds of ac-tions that the presence of God's rule sponsors. They are not directly images of God but of humans, their triumphs and failures. Some-times the stories are told in an almost comic tone: a character who deserves it comes to a bad end; a "bumbler" stumbles upon a for-tune. Often Jesus leaves his stories unfinished. He gets a story going, shows us something we might not expect, and then turns to the audi-ence and asks: "Well, what do you think?" How a particular person interprets a parable often depends upon how he/she polishes off Je-sus' unanswered questions. Sometimes the evangelists help answer those questions by attaching other sayings and teachings of Jesus to the end of a parable or, as we saw with the Lucan love of neighbor, using another tradition to serve as the frame for the parable. Since Jesus' audiences included many different types of people, there were probably different responses to his parables as he told them.

The kinds of behavior that Jesus is suggesting are a sign of the rule of God [Piper:86f]. Yet we have also seen that that kind of be-havior is only possible for those who are willing to reject the kind of sensible accommodation to human "hardness of heart" or "the evils of the times" typical of both the proverbial traditions and the legal accommodations made by the Pharisees. The prophets had seen that there appeared to be something of a "misfit" between us humans and God's demands for justice, for compassion, for aiding the poor of the community, for peace, etc. Jeremiah (31:31–34; 32:37ff) envisaged a time when God's covenant would become part of human nature. Then the cycle of disobedience-punishment-restoration that had been the history of God's people would be broken. Evil would be de-stroyed and righteousness prevail as in the visions of Enoch. Or, as Ezekiel put it, God would change the human heart of stone for one of flesh (36:26; cf. 11:19). Jesus challenges all visions that accommodate to the pessimism of the world about the present state of human possibilities. He begins by refusing to accept their picture of evil as an enormous, overwhelming blight on the world. It is still quite subordinate to the presence of God. It is not a mark against God's righteousness that some people disobey his commandments; nor is it a danger for good people to live in the world with sinners (contrary to the Essenes who sought to keep themselves separate from sinners). Jesus sees no reason why the good people might not be "contaminating the sinners" with their goodness. As for the dynamics of envy, we will see how Jesus imaged that in the prodigal son. Finally, about those "new hearts," they are around for those who are able to look at the world in the right way. God's presence is there to make them possible. The parable is there to show us how to look.

STUDY QUESTIONS

1. Why is the connection between ethics and the vision of God fundamental to biblical ethics?

2. How does a neo-Marxist, an existential or a psychological interpretation of Jesus' love command bypass the question of God?

3. What are the three major functions that language performs? Give an example of a statement that fits each category from the biblical material we have studied.

4. Why is the "scale" of the metaphors that Jesus uses to speak about God and human actions important?

5. How does Jesus challenge a pessimistic view of human behavior?

4
THE PRODIGAL SON

Lk 15:11–32

Study the parable of the prodigal son. Notice the number of phrases and expressions that are repeated in the different sections of the story. We have typed the younger and elder brother episodes in parallel columns. Notice the parallels between the incidents. What do you think? Did the elder go into the house?

Introduction

There was a man who had two sons; and the younger of them said to his father, "Father, give me the share of the property that falls to me." And he divided his living between them. Not many days later, the younger son gathered all he had and took his journey into a far country, and there he squandered his property in loose living. And, when he had spent everything, a great famine arose in that country, and he began to be in want.

Younger Son	Elder Son
So he went and joined himself to one of the citizens of that country, who sent him into the fields to feed swine. And he would gladly have fed on the pods that the swine ate; and no one gave him anything. But when he came to himself, he said,	Now his elder son was in the field; and as he came and drew near to the house, he heard music and dancing.
How many of my father's servants have enough and bread and more, but I perish here with hunger. I	And he called one of the servants and asked what this meant. And he said to him, Your brother has come, and your father has killed the fatted calf, because he has received him safe and sound.

51

will arise and go to my father, and
say to him, "Father, I have sinned
against heaven and before you; I
am no longer worthy to be called
your son; treat me as one of your
hired servants.

And he arose and came to his father. But while he was yet at a distance,

his father saw him and had compassion, and ran, and embraced
him and kissed him.

And the son said to him, Father, I
have sinned against heaven and before you; I am no longer worthy to
be called your son.

But the father said to his servants,
Bring quickly the best robe and put
it on him; and put a ring on his
hand, and shoes on his feet; and
bring the fatted calf and kill it, and
let us eat and make merry;

for this my son was dead, and is
alive again; he was lost and is
found.

But he was angry and refused to go
in.

His father came out, and entreated
him,

but he answered his father, Lo,
these many years I have served
you, and I never disobeyed your
command; yet
you never gave me a kid, that I
might make merry with my friends.
But when this son of yours came,
who has devoured your living with
harlots, you killed the fatted calf
for him.

And he said to him, Son, you are
always with me, and all that is
mine is yours. It was fitting to
make merry and be glad, for this
your brother was dead, and is alive;
he was lost and is found.

The Prodigal Son as a Story about Sinners

Luke uses this story to defend Jesus against the charge that he
ate with "tax collectors and sinners." It is important to recognize
that that charge functioned as an emotive term; it was used to slander Jesus, and the Christian teaching by opponents. There is very little deliberate "eating with sinners" in Jesus' ministry [Walker]. Jews
commonly associated "Gentile" with "sinner." The person for whom

the prodigal worked would be a "Gentile sinner" because he kept swine. Doubtless his treatment of the boy was just what a Jewish audience would expect a "godless pagan" to do. The Jewish father's good treatment of his own servants contrasts favorably with the Gentile behavior. These observations remind us that "being a sinner" also had social dimensions. It was not simply a question of private, individual actions. Jews commonly associated sexual immorality with the Gentiles. Consequently, the audience would immediately assume that the boy had gone off to one of the Gentile cities and gotten into exactly the kind of trouble they might expect their own sons to get into if they left the confines of family and Judaism. Lk's Gentile readers did not necessarily share those associations, but they could see this parable as an image of the inclusiveness of God's mercy, which extended even to them.

The boy's request has legal parallels from the times. It was a way of keeping sons from fighting over inheritance after the father's death. The elder always inherited the land. When a property division such as this was made, the father could no longer sell the land without the elder's consent, though the father continued to be in charge of things. Thus, the elder is assured of his inheritance. Notice that his father reminds him of that fact. There is no reason to accuse either son of "dishonoring the father" as some exegetes try to do. The younger son's sin is his total abandonment of Judaism. "Swineherd" was one of the occupations which Jews thought put a person outside the people of Israel [Jeremias:129]. One could easily imagine a Jewish father approving the introduction to the story as a warning for younger sons not to try their fortunes in the alluring Gentile cities. One must also admit that the initial reaction of the righteous, elder son is a quite predictable envy of what appears to be quite unfair, preferential treatment. Such charges and counter-charges are not too different from experiences in our own family life. Every parent has been in the father's shoes. Every child has been one or the other of the brothers. We have to remember not to turn the father into God, the younger son into "sinners" and the elder into "Pharisees" and not to allegorize the parable into "God forgives sinners and Pharisees don't like it." The dynamics of the parable are really about all of us and our relationships. Both boys think they know the score. They both, in fact, agree as to what the younger deserves. What happens to upset the tale? Is the father just foolish in acting the way he does and creating resentment in the elder son [see Breech]?

The Prodigal Son and Stories about Brothers

We cannot get all of the overtones in this story unless we remember that it is more than a tale of the contemporary problems faced by elder and younger sons, though it is that. It is also a tale about two brothers. We have seen that relationships between hostile brothers are an important focus for Jewish teaching about "love of brother." That observation alone reminds us that this story is not just about God and sinners. It is about people and each other. There are striking parallels between this tale and the Joseph stories, especially stories like Joseph and Asenath, which hold Joseph up as the model for a Jew forced to live among the corruptions of a Gentile world. Joseph remains untainted by the excess luxury, banquets, and sexual immorality, though he is falsely accused of the latter. Because of his righteousness and "love of enemy," God rescues him. Like Joseph, the boy is in a Gentile country at a time of severe famine, and is almost a slave in a Gentile's household. The father's gifts would also remind the audience of the Joseph story: shoes, robe, ring, banquet.

However, this boy is no Joseph. In fact, he is almost the parody of all the younger sons of folklore. The usual pattern has the younger son go off to seek his fortune, suffer adversity but maintain his integrity, cleverness, etc., achieve great success, and return home wealthier and more successful than any of his brothers. Such stories probably played an important role in building the confidence of younger sons who would be forced to go out and make their fortunes away from the family farm. But this boy is the anti-type of the successful younger son. He does everything that he should not do. Finally at the mid-point, the real beginning of the story of the father, he decides that the only course of action is to return home a failure. His reception, as the elder brother points out, befits a successful son, not a failed one.

The Prodigal Son as a Social Drama

One way of describing what happens in this story is to describe it as a "social drama," a story which plays out some of the tensions inherent in a society. Anthropologists use the term for rituals in which societies diffuse the tensions that build up by dramatizing them. This story is a carefully orchestrated whole, which should never be told without the concluding scene with the elder brother [Carlston]. The Lucan context provides a clue as to what the tension is all about. It is not just an invitation to sinners to repent, though the younger son provides a powerful image for the benefits that can come from repentance. It is also an invitation to the righteous, to the elder brother [Piper:82f]. Notice how carefully paralleled the two scenes are. They conclude with the same wording. The younger is met by the father "while still at a distance." The elder "came and drew near." Hunger brings the younger to his senses; the sounds of feasting causes the inquiry and anger of the elder. The "squandered property" and "famine" of the younger contrast with the "saved property" of the elder, and the father's remarks correlate these with images of life and death.

The father's action creates the problem. He must reconcile both sons. Remember, he can give a feast for the younger, but he can no longer give him any more property. Legally, that all belongs to the elder, as he tells him. The future of the younger may very much depend upon whether or not the father succeeds with the elder! And Jesus does not tell us that. What do you think? Can the father overcome the anger/envy of the elder brother? The key to Jesus' approach to the "envy of the righteous" reflected in this story is his insistence that rejoicing with the younger is both appropriate *and*

does not upset the relationship between the elder and the father. It remains as close as ever.

The younger son's actions evoked all the symbolic horrors of
sinfulness that Jewish imagination associated with the Gentiles. The
elder is exemplary in his devotion to duty. Neither understands the
father. This story suggests the tension that the righteous feel in the
presence of unmerited success of the wicked. We have seen the discussion of "envy" in the texts on non-retaliation present that theme.
This story takes a different approach. It hopes to persuade the righteous that they do not lose if they rejoice with the returning younger
son. They can perhaps come to see that the dynamics of envy is inappropriate.

Not surprisingly, this parable is a gold mine for those who wish
to give a psychological interpretation of Jesus' message. In Freudian
terms, the younger can be taken to represent the libido, which knows
no moral restraints; the elder, the super-ego's rigid adherence to
duty; the father, the necessary ability of a healthy adult ego to medi-
ate between the two. Others point to the importance of this parable
for a proper understanding of God. The God image is often internal-
ized as a harsh, demanding father. The elder son is a spokesperson
for that view. It is also the view which the righteous who demand
that God judge the world and vindicate their position have. Critics of
Christianity have castigated it for fostering such "cosmic resentment" of the righteous. However, Jesus' consciousness of God must
be quite different. His story points to human situations in which the
rigid consistency demanded of God by "the righteous" would be
much less appropriate than the behavior born of the father's compassion. The father need not be a direct allegory for God in order for the
story to require that we change our image of God.

However, such a psychological interpretation is not likely to
have been part of the original significance of the parable. But, its dynamics were played out often enough in the social dynamics of the
community. Lk sees it as Jesus vs. the Pharisees. That is not the only
tension that might have been provoked by his ministry. The Gospels

susggest that Jesus' disciples were not above worrying about the reward they would receive from following him; they were not above asking for positions of honor either. This story addresses that sort of tension just as effectively as it addresses the tension between Jesus and the righteous of Israel. It recognizes the "felt inequality" between righteous and sinners, yet it demands that the righteous put aside envy and demands for judgment to join in the rejoicing.

Beyond the social dynamics which this parable addresses, it makes a poignant comment on Jesus' own activity. On the one hand, it shows a clear recognition that compassion shown the sinner or outsider may have a negative backlash in the righteous who feel that their hard won gains are being undermined. Certainly, Jesus faced such reactions in his own ministry. The Christian reader, including the evangelist, knows that Jesus was not successful in reconciling hostile parties. Sometimes that recognition has led to identification of the elder with those who opposed Jesus or with those Jews who rejected early Christian preaching. This can lead to the false assumption that the story condemns the elder brother. Nothing could be further from the truth. The parable asserts the father's unity with the elder in as strong terms as it insists on the appropriateness of his treatment of the younger. By doing so, it leaves open the possibility for the elder to go in and rejoice. Neither son is permitted to score a victory over the other. That lesson is, perhaps, the hardest one we have to apply when we are trying to create our own reconciliations between opposing groups.

STUDY QUESTIONS

1. How would a Jewish reader in the first century evaluate the behavior of the younger son? Of the elder one?

2. What other Old Testament stories or folkstories about younger sons do you know? How do they turn out? How is Jesus' story similar? How is it different?

3. If what happens in this story is also a key to what God is like, what do we learn about God? About compassion?

4. Describe two different types of tension between people pictured in the story. How does the story envision resolving those tensions?

5. What do you think the elder brother did?

5
THE GOOD SAMARITAN

Lk 10:30–36

Study the parable of the good Samaritan. Lk has used it to illustrate the meaning of neighbor in the double love command. As in the previous parable, the Samaritan acts out of compassion. How does his action compare with that of the father in the prodigal son?

A man was going down from Jerusalem to Jericho, and he fell among robbers, who stripped him and beat him, and departed, leaving him half dead.

Now, by chance, a priest was going down that road; and when he saw him, he passed by on the other side.

So likewise, a Levite, when he came to the place and saw him, passed by on the other side.

But a Samaritan, as he journeyed, came to where he was; and when he saw him, he had compassion, and went to him and bound up his wounds, pouring oil and wine on them; then he set him on his own beast and brought him to an inn, and took care of him. And, the next day, he took two denarii and gave them to the innkeeper, saying, "Take care of him; and whatever more you spend, I will repay you when I come back."

Which of these three, do you think, proved neighbor to him who fell among robbers?

[Lk 10:30–36]

The Samaritan: Neighbor or Enemy?

This parable illustrates the term "neighbor" in the love of neighbor command in Lk. However, Jews and Samaritans were hostile to each other, so the original may have dealt with the question of enmity as well. The lawyer's question "Who is my neighbor?" which forms the introduction to the parable in Lk 10:29 represents a common debate in Hellenistic Jewish circles. How far does "neighbor" extend? Does it include anyone with whom a person has dealings even if that person is not Jewish? For Lk's Gentile community, the enmity between Samaritans and Jews would not have any significance [Berger:103f]. Lk's use of the parable is entirely appropriate for an audience which is no longer faced with the social dynamics engendered when two hostile groups live side by side as the Samaritans and Jews did in the first century (and as West Bank Palestinians and Jews do today). The application to love of neighbor is also appropriate because the original parable clearly erases all barriers to love and compassion, including that of enemy. The Samaritan treats the person he has least in common with as his "best friend" or relative. That's what the love command at its most radical implies.

However, Jesus' audience knew of a situation of real enmity between Samaritans and Jews. The original parable loses some of its dynamics and critical force when it is taken out of that situation [Piper:94f]. Even though both Samaritans and Jews kept to themselves, contacts between the two groups were necessary. The key pilgrimage routes between Galilee and Jerusalem lay through Samaria. Despite the Mosaic roots of Samaritan religious belief, they were considered Gentiles when it came to access to the temple. The two groups did not always interact violently. Historians report one serious incident of hostility between the two groups during the period of political breakdown prior to the Jewish revolt against Rome. The incident occurred in A.D. 48–52 [Freyne:73–76]. According to the Roman historian Tacitus, bands of robbers from both Galilee and Samaria engaged in raiding each other's villages. The Romans finally had to intervene [Ann. xii,54]. The Jewish historian Josephus reports two versions of an incident under the same procurators, which seems to have been the real cause of the Roman intervention [War ii,233–46; Ant xx,118–36]. What seems to have happened is that a Galilean pilgrim was murdered as he passed through a Samaritan village on his way to Jerusalem for the Passover. A band of his fellow Galileans, who were already in Jerusalem, went out and attacked the Samaritan village. Josephus suggests that the violence spilled over into other Samaritan villages as well, but historians are not sure that this is really what happened. The Samaritans appealed to the Syrian legate, who ignored the plea. Finally, he had to intervene, which he did by executing some of those involved and sending others to Rome. Ant xx,136 claims that the Samaritans were finally found guilty of starting the incident and their leaders were executed. Another individual is sent back to Jerusalem for public torture and execution. Tacitus, on the other hand, only says that some Jews who had killed Roman soldiers were executed.

All these versions depend upon the particular view of the Jewish revolt and its causes held by the historian in question. The following facts do appear to be clear. A single Jewish pilgrim is murdered in Samaria—perhaps by a band of robbers as happens in Jesus' parable. The incident provoked some form of lawless retaliation against a Samaritan village by a band of Galilean Jews, who had apparently been told of the incident by other travelers. This type of Jewish retaliation is reflected in a comment in Lk 9:51, where the disciples ask Jesus to call down divine vengeance on a Samaritan village that refuses them hospitality. Such lesser expressions of violent feelings between the two groups were probably the normal experience of Galilean pilgrims. In Jn 4:9 a Samaritan woman answers Jesus' request for water by reminding Jesus of the hostility between the two groups. (Notice that the evangelist has expanded her remark to provide an explanation for Samaritan Jewish hostility. The grounds for such Samaritan refusal are also reflected in Jn.) During the hostilities between the two groups, which broke out in Maccabean times because the Sa-

maritans refused to adopt the Jerusalem cult and to reject the Helle-
nizing policies of the Seleucid rulers, the Jews came and burned the
Samaritan temple (in 128 B.C.; Jn 4:20 refers to the conflict over
place of worship). As far as one can tell, the Jews generally had the
upper hand in terms of violence and political power. The Samaritans
might express their resentment by refusing to aid Jewish pilgrims.
Certainly they would not be expected to feel any compassion for one
who had fallen victim to robbers on the road! They would probably
argue that they had suffered more at the hands of the Jews than they
had ever given out. Thus, the hostility inherent in the situation presupposed by Jesus' parable is clearly one of enmity.

The Enemy Becomes the Loving Neighbor

The audience who hears a parable makes a great deal of difference to its interpretation. One of the earliest missions outside Judaism was to Samaria. Samaritan and Gentile Christians might hear
this story as one of praise for their conversion as well as a general
call for mercy on anyone in need.

The reactions of Jesus' original, Jewish audience would have
been considerably more complex. The anti-clericalism of many twentieth century interpreters should be rejected. It is likely that they
would have assumed that the priest and Levite were both honoring
ritual laws that forbade contact with a corpse, even though the Levite was not strictly obligated to do so if he was on his way back to
his village after finishing his turn at the temple. Perhaps they had
even seen such examples. Both are treated in stylized fashion. The
double stroke of bad luck merely heightens the tension over whether
the man will be rescued. That tension would be very much height-
ened as soon as the Samaritan appeared on the horizon. If Samaritans refuse water to thirsty Jewish pilgrims, they certainly would not
pull one out of a ditch! Further, the Jews also appear to have used
the term "Samaritan" of other Jews whom they wished to insult,
much as certain racial or ethnic epithets can be used to insult a per-

son of one's own group today. (This insult is slung at Jesus in Jn 8:48.) Thus, in telling such a story to a Jewish audience, Jesus' Samaritan character would invoke the image of a person who would certainly ignore the man. Further, the derogatory use of "Samaritan" as an epithet among Jews suggests that they considered Samaritans morally and religiously inferior. Such a person could only function as a negative example. A person who did not fit the standards of the Jewish community might be called "Samaritan."

The Samaritan in Jesus' story, then, almost becomes a counter-example of the kind of violence we read about in Josephus. The parable focuses our attention on the Samaritan's compassionate behavior by describing it in great detail. He goes way beyond the minimum needed to save the man's life. He makes an extraordinary expenditure of his personal assets in helping the man and making sure that he will recover. Such behavior completely finesses the legal question of how far one has to extend love of neighbor. One would hardly do more if the man in the ditch had been a close friend or family, let alone an enemy.

One can hardly capture all the issues this story must have triggered in the minds of Jesus' audience. On the one hand, the man has behaved in the most exemplary manner possible. On the other, what has happened to all the realities of life that "every Galilean knows" about Samaritans? Not only is it almost inconceivable that a Samaritan would aid a Jew; what is perhaps even worse is that Jesus has taken a despised Samaritan and made him an example for a Jewish audience of the highest fulfillment of the law imaginable. How can the morally inferior Samaritan practice such compassion? Clearly, the parable has challenged a complex set of social responses. The Samaritan seems to behave as though the whole history of hatred between the two groups never existed. One suspects that the standard stories about Samaritans among Galilean pilgrims were more like Lk 9:51 or Jn 4:9 than they were like this story. What do you imagine the Jew said when he found out that a Samaritan had rescued him?

Certainly, this parable deals with the problem of love of enemies at its very roots. It deals with those enemies created and reinforced by the social groups of hostile neighbors—neighbors whose hostilities are grounded in religious differences. It places the Jewish audience in the position of conflicting reactions. Several points made in the story are quite clear, however:

1. Love is not a command that is addressed to persons who are materially disadvantaged, who have to "love" their enemies/masters in order to survive. The Samaritan envisaged appears to be fairly well off, perhaps a traveling merchant.

2. The whole question of "who" is neighbor and "how far" do I have to go misses the point. One does not calculate, not even friend or enemy. The man is treated as if he were a "best friend." Nothing is calculated; nothing is too much.

3. The Samaritan had no reason to aid this person. If anything, the history of Samaritan-Jewish relations would make a strong case against it. After all, the Jews do not respect his Mosaic ancestry; they treat him as a Gentile and use his name as a "dirty word" among themselves. One might even wonder what the Samaritan's friends would have thought of his action!

Like the prodigal son, then, this parable shows compassion as something which sets up rather a puzzle. It ignores social boundaries and all the reasonable sorts of calculations that people make. It may even cause those who are recipients or witnesses of it some perplexity. Such love is a long way from the sweet "Love conquers all" viewpoint that is sometimes attributed to Christianity. These parables show that Jesus understands compassion and love of enemy to be very complex problems. But he does not think that it is necessary to wait until the end of the world to see love in action. Concrete, particular instances of this love can occur anywhere at any time with the most surprising people as examples of it.

Both the prodigal son and the good Samaritan challenge Jesus' audience to question some of the prejudices they have about the way the world is. Some people in the audience might have known a father something like the prodigal's; perhaps one or two had received some form of unexpected aid from a Samaritan. Those who knew people who had been injured by Samaritans would never believe such a story, and local prejudice would certainly be skeptical. Who knows what any who had been involved in retaliation against Samaritans would have felt; perhaps they would have defended themselves by attacking Jesus. In any case, the concluding question makes the audience acknowledge that the Samaritan is both "good" and "compassionate" and that even a Samaritan can be an example of the greatest mercy possible!

STUDY QUESTIONS

1. How is the compassion of the good Samaritan like that of the father in the parable of the prodigal son?

2. Describe the causes of enmity between Samaritans and Jews.

3. What does this story tell the lawyer about the extent of the term "neighbor"?

4. What objections do you think Jesus' audience might have raised as he was telling this story? What do you think he would have told them?

5. What do you think the Jew told his friends about the incident? What do you think the Samaritan told his friends?

6
LOVE AND THE CHRISTIAN CONSCIENCE

1 Cor 8:1–13; 10:23–11:1

The following passages deal with a very peculiar crisis of conscience that afflicted Christians at Corinth. People argued over whether they could eat meat that had been sacrificed to idols. The passages in italics represent slogans that people were using. See if you can figure out how Paul has changed their slogans.

Now about food offered to idols:
We know that *all of us possess knowledge.* Knowledge puffs up, but love builds up. If anyone imagines that he knows something, he does not yet know as he ought to know. But, if one loves God, one is known by him.

Hence, as to eating food offered to idols:
We know that *an idol has no real existence.* And, *there is no God but one.* For although there may be so-called gods in heaven or on earth—as indeed there are many "gods" and "lords"—yet *for us there is one God,* the Father from whom all things come and for whom we exist, and one Lord, Jesus Christ, through whom all things come and through whom we exist.

However, not all possess this knowledge. But some, through being previously accustomed to idols, eat food as really offered to an idol. And their conscience, being weak, is defiled.

Food will not commend us to God. We are no worse off if we do not eat and no better off if we do. Only take care lest this liberty of yours somehow become a stumbling block to the weak. For if anyone sees you, a man of knowledge, at a table in an idol's temple, might he not be encouraged, if his conscience is weak, to eat food offered to idols? And so, by your knowledge, this weak man is destroyed, the brother for whom Christ died. Thus, sinning against your brethren and wounding their conscience when it is weak, you sin against Christ.

Therefore, if food is the cause of my brother's falling, I will never eat meat, lest I cause my brother to fall.

[1 Cor 8:1–13]

All things are lawful. But not all things are helpful.

All things are lawful. But not all things build up. Let no one seek his own good but the good of his neighbor.

Eat whatever is sold in the meat market without raising any question on the ground of conscience, for "the earth is the Lord's and everything in it."

If an unbeliever invites you to dinner and you are disposed to go, eat whatever is set before you without raising any question of conscience.

But if someone says to you, "This has been offered in sacrifice," then out of consideration for the man who informed you, and for conscience' sake—I mean his conscience, not yours—do not eat it.

For, *why should my liberty be determined by another man's scruples? If I partake with thankfulness, why am I denounced because of that for which I give thanks?*

So, whatever you eat and drink, or whatever you do, do all to the glory of God. Give no offense to Jews or to Greeks or to the church of God, just as I try to please all men in everything I do, not seeking my own advantage, but that of many that they may be saved.

Be imitators of me as I am of Christ.

[1 Cor 10:23–11:1]

Conscience as a Moral Guide in Antiquity

Conscience as it is used in moral philosophers of the time was essentially negative and was responsive to the standards of the community. When an individual's behavior was out of line with the common norms, his conscience would indicate that fact by afflicting him [Bultmann:210ff]. Early Christians adopted this view along with other ethical traditions from their culture (as in Rom 2:15). Jewish traditions also have this picture of conscience (Wis 17:11; TReub iv,3). Sometimes conscience is presented as a motivation superior to fear of judgment (Rom 13:5; see Kaesemann:358). Lack of bad conscience could be appealed to in forensic situations as evidence for the truth or integrity of the defendant's claims. Paul uses the expression in this way in Rom 9:1. (Kaesemann:64–66, holds that the expression should not be "over-interpreted" to imply that Christians practiced examination of conscience, against Schlier:79.) When he is challenged, Paul appeals to conscience as testimony to the integrity of his apostolic work (2 Cor 1:12; 4:2; 5:11; similarly 2 Tim 1:3).

The conventional moral teaching held that conscience increased the torments of the wicked. Wis 17:10 uses it to interpret the torments of the Egyptians. TReub iv,3 has conscience torment the impious person. Philo intensified the legal overtones of conscience by using the term *elenchos* (interrogation or proof leading to conviction) as its equivalent [Winston:307f]. Conscience belongs to the reasoning faculty and represents an innate knowledge of good and evil (Deus 50; Fug 131, as a general guide). As an internal judge, conscience records the soul's transgressions and inflicts punishment by causing the individual to suffer (Deus 126; Op 128; Det 22–32; Jos 47f). Souls that are so far from reason that they sin without knowing it are unable to act morally until "right reason," like a high priest, has entered the soul, cleansing and healing it (Deus 133–38; 182f). This internal high priest keeps the soul from going astray (Fug 117f). Consequently, "good conscience" meant that nothing was troubling an individual internally. (Horsley suggests that we should translate "conscience" as "consciousness" in order to capture this meaning: 1978a:581ff.)

When early Christian preaching encouraged Christians to have a good conscience (1 Pt 2:19; 3:16), it was using the word in its common sense. The person who is obedient to moral norms will have a good conscience, especially since that person has given up the evils of paganism (1 Pt 3:21). Salvation can even be described as having a good conscience (Heb 13:18). We saw that Philo gave conscience a liturgical setting tied to the "cleansing" action of reason as high priest. Early Christians did the same. The epistle to the Hebrews, which shows many other links to the kind of traditions represented in Philo, associates the cleansed Christian conscience with the purifying from sins that came through the death of Jesus, the heavenly high priest (9:14; 10:22). He argues that Jewish atonement rituals were unable to purify conscience (9:9; 10:2).

The pastoral epistles extend the injunction to have a good conscience to "holding the faith" against other Christians whose teachings and practices the author considers heretical (1 Tim 1:5,9; 3:9; 4:2f, against some who would forbid marriage and enjoin abstinence from certain foods). Conscience will convict such individuals (Tit 1:15). The particular features of the heresy involved are not clear. The practices involved may have been a kind of asceticism and withdrawal from the world that Paul is already rejecting in 1 Cor. However, the use of "conscience" in these writings accords with the conventional one. The author has simply added certain Christian conventions to the general moral sense of the community at large.

However, precisely because conscience was so linked to the general moral sense of the community, it could cause problems for Christians whose very conversion caused them to break with some of the traditions and mores of that community, with family and friends. The controversy over eating idol meat is an example of just such a problem. For some, even eating meat that was being sold in the market after having been used in a sacrifice at one of the temples was too close to the "idolatry" from which they had come. They found their consciences tormenting them. Others had no such difficulty. Christians also found that their own intense ideals of perfection raised problems of conscience as we shall see in the last chapter. 1 Cor 8:3 is a phrase which may have been used to reassure such people that as long as they stayed within the community and continued to "love God" and one another, they need not worry about torments of conscience. God, not conscience, is finally in charge of the judgment and salvation of each person. For Paul conscience is not the central theme of Christian ethics. Its use as a term is borrowed from contemporary moral teaching. It may have been introduced into the discussion by the Corinthians rather than by the apostle. He insists that Christians derive their ethical guidance from revelation, from what has happened in Christ. Love which stems from faith is the key moral quality [Houlden:17–31].

The Christian of Weak Conscience

Outside of the Pauline context, weakness of conscience seems to emerge over against Christian perfectionism. Christians commit sins after baptism, which need not separate them from all hope of salvation (1 Pt 4:8, Jas 5:20b, both quoting Prov 10:12; see Göppelt:283–85). Generally, realization that salvation was not completely lost took the form of "God is greater than" statements. 1 Pt 4:8 has "love covers sins," that is, love of neighbor/enemy. 1 Jn, which was engaged in a severe struggle over perfectionism, [Bogart; Perkins, 1979], reassures its readers with: "Even if our hearts condemn us, God is greater than our hearts" (1 Jn 3:19–24). A similar expression appears in 1 Cor 8:3. Paul is using it to reassure Christians whose conscience troubles them.

The exact issues in the idol meat controversy are not clear. Jews had a strong aversion to eating meat that had been used in sacrifices to idols, so some exegetes think that the objections came from Jewish Christians. However, such Christians would have continued to observe kosher practices and would not have been in the position to observe and object to the practices of other Christians. Paul is not making allowance for Christians who wanted to attend banquets in temples that sometimes followed such an animal sacrifice. That is forbidden outright in 1 Cor 10:1–22. The issue in these passages is whether the Christian can eat meat which had been used in a sacrifice and was being sold in the market.

Paul's debate with the Corinthians over this issue and the argument about conscience that was apparently going on between both sides in Corinth is the only sustained treatment of conscience in the New Testament. Stendahl treats the issues involved under the provocative "catch phrase": "Love rather than integrity" [1976:61–67]. Both those who ate idol meat, "the strong," and those who refused, "the weak," were appealing to conscience. The weak used the torments of their own conscience as an indication that eating such meat was wrong, and that anyone who did so must be acting in bad conscience. The strong insisted that their conscience did not bother them and that they had good theological reasons (knowledge) for not worrying about such meat, since they knew that there was only one God. Paul will insist that conscience fails as a guide in this situation [Furnish:229]. The norms of Christian love as Paul understands them override the claims of individual conscience, since the latter does not properly express the interpersonal demands of ethical action. The individual may be "right" in that he/she is acting out of full conviction of his/her conscience and yet wrong because of its effect on the other members of the community [Horsley:586–88].

Paul accepts the theological principle advocated by the strong that since the idols are not really gods, eating the meat is not relevant to one's religious status. But he does not want that principle to become the downfall of Christians whose conscience troubles them when faced with idol meat. The argument advanced by the strong and Paul's acceptance of it depend upon the preaching of monotheism to the Gentiles. This belief was formulated in statements about the true principle behind the universe such as that in 1 Cor 8:6, which adopts the Jewish picture of God and his word or wisdom as the foundation of the universe to the Christian picture of God and Christ. Paul has apparently appended that traditional doxological formula to the slogan being used by the strong in order to remind them that "knowledge" does not put them outside subjection to the Lord. Paul has already begun to specify what that "subjection" means for all Christians when he introduces love in 8:3 [Horsley, 1978b; 1980/81]. The building up of the community through love will be the fundamental principle by which Paul tries to turn the arguments of both sides away from the general, universal principles and slogans being thrown at each other to a genuinely Christian perception of obligation.

Love for the Brother as the Limit to Christian Freedom

As soon as he introduces the issue of conscience, Paul makes it clear that the troubled conscience of the weak is the focus of his concern. The "knowledge" of the strong has no value if the community is destroyed as a result of their action. 1 Cor 8:7 suggests that the weak are not Jewish Christians but converts from paganism who are unable to shake the feeling that their former "gods and lords" have some reality.

"Food will not commend us to God" (8a) was probably also a slogan from Christian missionary preaching. It represented the Christian freedom from Jewish food laws. Some exegetes think that the whole verse represents an argument that the strong used against the weak. "We," they argue, refers to the strong. They are claiming against the weak that their "spiritual gifts" prove that eating idol meat has no religious significance. They are no "better off" (when it comes to speaking in tongues, prophesying, etc.) when they abstain from such meat and no worse off when they eat it [Murphy-O'Connor, 1979]. Others, who hold that 8b,c are the apostle's addition interpret the expression as referring to both groups. The weak are not "better off" for abstaining; the strong are not "worse off" for eating such meat [Conzelmann:147]. That formulation, as you doubtless noticed, states the issue as it would have appeared from the standpoint of the weak, who claimed to be "better off" for not eating such meat. But though the meat itself may be indifferent, the rest of the passage seeks to show that the act of eating is not indifferent.

Paul replaces the theistic argument of his opponents with one that is specifically Christian in vv 9–13. Salvation does not come from the monotheistic insight, which Christians in any case shared with others, but from Christ's death on behalf of the weak. Since the action of the strong destroys the weak, it is more than a failure of love; it is a sin against Christ himself. Paul acknowledges the fact that the weak cannot help the torments of conscience. The tormenting action of a troubled conscience is quite real enough. But that torment itself does not give the weak an argument against the strong. Thus, it is very clear that Paul is not telling the strong to capitulate to the conclusions that the weak draw from their tormented conscience—far from it.

The question which the strong have to ask is of a different order. It concerns the effect of the act of eating. The Christian is perfectly free to eat such meat. However, when doing so would destroy another person, for whom Christ died, the Christian will forego the exercise of that liberty so that such a person will not be lost. The salvation of the weak is at stake. Paul sets out the issues in this debate in his own terms (notice that he talks about conviction rather than conscience when he does so) in Rom 14:1–15:6. When he speaks of the Christian willingness to bear one another's burdens (15:1–6), he attributes the principle of being guided by the need of the other person to Christ.

Clearly, Paul does not think that the theological arguments of the strong justify imposing their view on the weak even though it is correct. The question remains whether and how the conscience of the weak might be changed. We have seen that principles like that in 1 Cor 8:3 were sometimes evoked in cases of troubled conscience. The second section of the argument may be a more extended presentation of principles which Paul hopes can change the situation.

Guidelines for the Corinthians To Follow

1 Cor 10:23–11:1 contains some general guidelines that Christians can follow in dealing with the idol meat question. Paul introduces the section with a slogan of the strong, "All things are lawful," which he modifies. Then he concludes the introduction with the general principle guiding his actions as an apostle (as he has just argued in ch. 9) and his advice to the Corinthians: "Let no one seek his own good but the good of his neighbor." This principle may have been a common form of the preaching of the love command. Paul will remind the readers of his apostolic example at the conclusion of the chapter, when he makes a characteristic appeal to imitate him as he does Christ [Furnish:220].

The first principle, to eat anything sold in the market without worrying about it (v 24), is backed up with another appeal to God's sovereignty as Creator.

The second principle (v 25) introduces a new situation. What about invitations to meals from pagan friends? Such invitations might have involved important social occasions such as weddings and funerals. A later Christian writing has a mother who had converted to Christianity refusing to eat with her son and his friends [Clem. Hom. XIII 4; Murphy-O'Connor, 1978b:552–55]. Paul has already told the Corinthians that he does not favor a Christian isolationism from contacts with non-Christians (5:9f; 7:13f). He has also already told them that they cannot accept invitations to banquets held in a pagan temple, but, for the rest, if the Christian wishes to accept the invitation, he can do so without raising any questions.

The third case (vv 26–29) is somewhat vague. It is not clear who the informant is or the circumstances under which the remark is made. Some interpreters assume that it must be one of the weak who is also at the banquet. Others doubt that the weak would have accepted and presume that the informant might have been a pagan friend. The party does not matter. Paul repeats his principle: the conscience of the person who gives that information is to be one's guide.

Verses 29b–30 may provide a further clue as to the general argument behind the controversy. They also take up a possible objection to Paul's principle [Murphy-O'Connor, 1978b:555–71]. The general practice of blessing food may have been part of the argument made by the strong for their freedom to eat anything. Both it and Paul's "Do all for the glory of God" derive from Judaism [cf. Rom 14:6; Leitzmann:53f]. Against the objections raised by the weak, the strong point out that they too bless the food they eat, and that they eat it in good conscience.

This sequence of principles can be seen as an attempt to formulate behavior that both groups should recognize as legitimate. However, the question of changing behavior applies differently to the two groups. Paul does want the weak to recognize that the strong give thanks to God and are not acting out of bad conscience [Murphy-O'Connor:564–73]. The strong are explicitly required to change, since they should recognize a higher obligation to the building up of the community which comes from Christ as the source of salvation and divine election [Murphy-O'Connor, 1978a]. Freedom in the Christian sense does not assert the rights of an autonomous individual but looks to the need of the weaker members so that the whole community will be built up. Such freedom is ultimately grounded in the action of Christ, which is concerned with the weak. Paul introduces the apostolic "imitatio" as the norm for such behavior.

The argument does not conclude that the weak can change in the same way. Attempts to do so on the part of the strong have simply led to sloganizing recriminations on both sides. Paul begins by applying the theistic principle as broadly as he can. In situations not directly connected with the pagan temple, one need not be concerned about how the meat was slaughtered. The ambiguous third principle may have intended to enlist the weak on the side of the strong. Paul uses a vague "someone" and has the informant use the pagan term "hierothyton," "sacrificial meat," rather than the Jewish and Christian "idol meat." Thus, he may well have a pagan informant in mind [so Conzelmann:177f]. If so, Paul is providing a case in which the principle of the weak, "Never eat idol meat," could be accepted as the norm for all Christians. Don't do it when a pagan makes an issue of it (lest he question the sincerity of your conversion). The troubled conscience is now shifted onto the pagan informant. Paul may hope that this shift will allow the weak to see that the really troubled conscience is not his own but that of a pagan who might be misled by one's behavior. The final principle, "giving thanks," should also include both groups. They are to give thanks and to seek the salvation of all others. Thus, it is possible to see this passage as an attempt to educate the conscience of the weak by reorienting its concerns. The real question is how the community stands with others. This evangelical emphasis emerges when Paul points back to his own apostolic example. Missionary activity and apostolic example are an important part of the building up of the community that Paul has in mind. He is not just telling the strong to capitulate to pressure from the weak for the sake of untroubled social harmony [Murphy-O'Connor:273; 1 Cor 14:3,24,26; Paul's own mission must be borne out in the testimony given by his congregations, Phil 2:14–26; 1 Th 3:2–8].

Thus, to speak of a Christian conscience, one must see that it is qualified by two concerns: love of the weak brother for whom Christ died; concern for the non-Christian to whom the Christian must bear witness. Christ's death "for the weak" is a direct example of the first; his lowliness, suffering and humility as it is mediated by the example of the missionary apostle serves as an example of the second. Paul's approach to the weak conscience is also instructive. He does not deny the objectivity of the pain felt by such people. However, he suggests that it might be alleviated indirectly, through incorporation into the larger context of Christian witness. Paul does present some simple rules for both sides. He refuses to accept the hostile recriminations of either group. Finally, he seeks to enlist them both in the common thanksgiving to God, the common "imitatio" of his apostolic example, and the common concern for the external witness that they must bear among the pagans. Both sides must be united in glorifying God.

STUDY QUESTIONS

1. How was conscience understood in the moral teaching of antiquity?

2. Give two examples from the New Testament in which Christians simply use the common understanding of conscience.

3. Why did some Christians find that they had a problem with "weak conscience"? How was that problem answered?

4. Write a brief dialogue between a weak and strong Christian at Corinth which brings out the theological position of each side. Which side do you think that you would have been on?

5. State Paul's answer to each side. What do you think the strong would have said in response to Paul? What do you think the weak would have said?

6. How does Paul use the example of Christ to provide the basis for Christian behavior? What understanding of conscience does he challenge in setting out his Christian principles?

7
LOVE AS CHRISTIAN FREEDOM

Gal 5:13–24

Study the following passage from Galatians. How does love's relation to Christian freedom in this passage compare with Paul's principles in 1 Cor 8–10? Paul has built this passage on an opposition symbolized by "flesh" and "spirit." Make a list of what belongs under each category.

For you, my brothers, were called to freedom. Only, do not let this freedom become an opportunity for the flesh, but through love become slaves of one another.

For the whole law is fulfilled in one word: You shall love your neighbor as yourself. If, however, you bite one another and tear each other to pieces, make sure you are not consumed by one another.

But, I say, walk by the Spirit, and you will not carry out the desire of the flesh. For the flesh sets its desires against the Spirit, and the Spirit against the flesh, since they are opposed to each other, so that you do not do the things which you intend. If, however, you are led by the Spirit you are not under the law.

The works of the flesh are evident, such things as sexual immorality, impurity, licentiousness, idolatry, sorcery, hostilities, strife, jealousy, outbursts of anger, quarrels, dissensions, factions, outbreaks of envy, cases of drunkenness, excessive banquets and things like these. In regard to these

I warn you as I have warned you before, "Those who do such things will not inherit the kingdom of God."

But the fruit of the Spirit is: love, joy, peace, forbearance, kindness, goodness, faithfulness, humility, self-control. No law is against such things! But those who belong to Christ have crucified their flesh with its passions and desires.

[Gal 5:13–24]

The Struggle for Christian Freedom

The immediate problem facing Paul in Galatia was the possibility that his young, Gentile Church might be won over by Jewish Christian preachers into following the law. Paul is consistently arguing that Gentile Christians can belong to the people of God without coming under the law [Stendahl, 1976]. However, this position derived from his perception that the law was not the source of salvation. For both Jew and Gentile, salvation had to come through faith in Christ. It did not mean that the kind of behavior presented in the ethical teachings of the law was bad, or that Christians could do anything they chose.

However, the preaching of Christian freedom does seem to have caused considerable turmoil in Pauline churches. In the Church at Corinth, interpretation of Christian freedom spilled over into some bizarre behavior. Some interpreters think that similar problems beset Galatia [Schlier:241f, who rightly points to Paul's combination of his ethical teaching and his rejection of the Jewish Christian position as a way of showing that the Galatians had departed quite some distance from what they were taught]. However, Paul does not give us any indications of that sort of behavior. The vices in this passage come from a stock catalogue. It may be that the Galatians were simply confused about proper Christian behavior and the failures of Christians. The law was probably seen by the Jewish Christians, as it commonly was among Hellenistic Jews, as an enlightened moral guide. Perhaps, the Galatians felt that by "entering the covenant with Abraham" through circumcision and keeping at least some part of the law, they would find a way to deal with human sinfulness [Betz:417]. They certainly would not have thought that such a move would forfeit the salvation they had in Christ or be like returning to the slavery of paganism as Paul argues in chapters 3 and 4. The Galatians need to recognize that the "cutting edge" of Christian ethics is freedom. That freedom is only preserved by walking in the Spirit. Such behavior can only manifest what is good. It does not leave any room for evil. Paul also makes it clear that walking in the Spirit means living as a member of the believing community (cf. 6:15; Betz:32f).

Love Fulfills the Law

When Paul speaks about freedom and walking in the Spirit, he is expressing the eschatological side of Christian ethics. He is not claiming that this freedom is something inherent in human nature. Rather, the gift of the Spirit, the power of God, which is now available to the believer since the coming of salvation in Christ, makes this freedom possible [Furnish:211–15]. Paul insists that the experience of the Spirit which people associated with the messianic age (after the obliteration of evil in Jewish apocalypses) is now present. The Christian does not live entirely under the rules of the "old, evil age" in which the law was necessary to keep the people of God in line. (Compare Paul's picture of the presence of the new age with Jesus' presence of the kingdom of God. Christian ethics is never simply read out of the conditions of the "present age.") At the same time, Gal 5 makes it quite clear that the presence of the Spirit does not mean that all Christians are suddenly perfect. Evil has not yet been destroyed. The freedom that the Christian enjoys can still be corrupted by the flesh. Hence, there is always a tension in Pauline ethics between the presence of salvation and the necessary exhortation to Christians to live out of that salvation.

The connection between freedom and salvation dominates both the theological and the ethical argument of Gal (e.g., 3:13; 4:4). Verse 13a is parallel to 5:1a, which introduced the final summary of the theological argument. The rest of verse 13 makes it clear that the task of Christian ethics is to preserve the freedom won in salvation. Verses 13–15 present love as the key to that task. The Christian is presented with two alternative uses of freedom. Freedom can be used as an "opportunity for the flesh" or it can be the occasion to serve one another in love. The type of behavior associated with each option will be presented in the virtue and vice lists which make up the second section (vv 19–21; 22–23).

Verse 13c hints at the problem which has probably made the law attractive to the Galatians. They have come to see that sinfulness still remains a problem among Christians [Betz:273 n.1 against those who think that instances of anitnomian behavior were involved]. Paul will point to a procedure for dealing with the sins of Christians in 6:1. He also recognizes that his earlier argument that the law is not the way to reconciliation with God does not quite address this problem. In 5:6, he argued that salvation does not come through the law but only through Christ, through faith working through love. The expression "faith working through love" is apparently an adaptation of a Hellenistic Jewish maxim. We saw a version of it in Aristeas 229 where the answer to what resembled beauty in value was "piety, for it is the pre-eminent form of beauty and its power lies in love, which is the gift of God." Paul's formulation of the love of brother as "Become slaves of one another" brings together several levels of symbolism. It fits the earlier theological argument, since Paul told the Galatians that their desire to be under the law was a slavery equivalent to their former slavery to pagan gods. Paul also frequently uses the "slave" metaphor in exhortation. It is particularly appropriate for the imitation of Christ who took on the "form of a slave" (Phil 2:7). It describes the apostolic ministry (Gal 1:10; Rom 1:1; Phil 1:1; 2:22; 1 Cor 9:19; 2 Cor 4:5), and the obedience of Christians generally (Rom 6:16; 7:6; 12:11; 14:18; 16:18; 1 Cor 7:21–23, which also addresses Christians who were really slaves; 1 Th 1:9).

Verse 14 makes the love of neighbor command the fulfillment of the whole law. That fulfillment would include the ritual commands of the law such as circumcision [Schlier:224; also the understanding of it that we saw in the pre-Markan tradition]. By beginning with the love command as fulfilling the whole law, Paul has cut off the possibility of instituting a Christian law. That possibility may have been what his opponent in Galatia had in mind [cf. 6:2; Betz:275]. Paul may have derived this use of the love command as a summary of the law from the Jesus tradition rather than from the Jewish examples [Schlier:245]. Rom 13:8–10 shows that it was a regular part of Pauline ethical teaching. In Rom, love is presented as fulfillment of the law in connection with examples from the decalogue. This combination is typical of both the Jewish examples and the Synoptic tradition. Some exegetes suggest that Paul has deliberately omitted any reference to the decalogue here in Gal so that he would not appear to be endorsing the position of his opponents. Instead, he uses more general moral exhortation. Verse 15 is such a general moral warning against backbiting, which compares such behavior to that of wild beasts. It was a common topic in moral preaching and is not an indication that the Galatians were any more or less prone to such behavior than the rest of humanity.

Contrast Between the Two Ways of Walking

Verses 16–23 contrast walking in the flesh and in the Spirit. The double catalogue of virtues and vices is a typical feature of such forms of ethical preaching. Paul argues that a person led by the Spirit hardly needs to be under the law, since the fruits of the Spirit far exceed anything that the law might command. The law can only function to restrain sin such as those in the list that he cites. Notice that most of the vices involved are social in nature. They are the kind of vice that destroys the community which it is Paul's (and every Christian's) aim to build up. The list of virtues is different from that in common Hellenistic sermons, since "fruits of the Spirit," "joy" and "peace" all point to the Christian life as one which is lived out of the presence of the new age.

Verse 24 summarizes the entire section with an appeal to the Christian to "crucify the flesh and its desires." Paul never turns such advice into a world-denying asceticism. The objects of that crucifixion are quite clearly indicated in the vice list. Verses 25 and 26 give general examples of what Paul has in mind.

Though love as fulfillment of the law and walking in the Spirit specify the basis of the ethical life of Christians, Paul does treat the problem of Christian sinfulness in 6:1–3. Thus, it is clear that he does not expect that Christians will somehow reform their behavior overnight. Such a procedure makes it possible for Christians to deal with brothers who do not walk in the Spirit without instituting a new law. Instead, they are to exhort (as Paul has just done) one another to walk in the Spirit. Gal 6:2 applies "love of brother" to his problem. Christians must "bear one another's burdens," that is, the failures of each member of the community. Verse 3 warns those who engage in such exhortation that they must be careful of their own conduct. Paul may have taken the expression "law of Christ" in v. 2b from his opponents. He now uses it to show that Christians, walking in the Spirit, fulfill the law in their love of one another [Betz:295–301]. Paul probably did not invent the suggestions he gives for dealing with erring Christians. It has a parallel in Jas 5:19f. Jas 5:20 adds that there is a twofold advantage in this way of dealing with the problem. First, the erring Christian is saved. Second, the sins of the person who brings back such a person are covered: "Love covers a multitude of sins" (Prov. 12:10; also 1 Pt 4:8).

Thus, Paul insists that it is possible to have a Christian ethic based on freedom, love, and walking in the Spirit. Christianity does not have to adopt the law or formulate a new equivalent for it. However, this approach places a certain obligation on the Christian community. Christians must constantly exhort one another to that love which fulfills the law. Of course, that love and walking in the Spirit are to bear fruits which can never be fully specified. The other New Testament examples of walking in the Spirit fill out what the new life of the Christian entails. They are always more encompassing than whatever could be established as law.

STUDY QUESTIONS

1. What is the theological basis for Christian freedom in Galatians?

2. What makes Paul's ethics different from that of the ethical preachers from whom he takes themes like his vice catalogue?

3. Why might the Galatian Christians have been attracted to the idea of adopting the law?

4. Why does Paul insist that Christians should not take on the law? Do you think the Galatians would have agreed?

5. Read Gal 6:1–3. How are Christians to deal with other Christians who sin? Do you think that that advice could still work today?

8
LOVE AS FULFILLMENT OF THE LAW

Jas 2:8–13

Study the passage on love of neighbor as the fulfillment of the Law below. How does it compare with Paul's treatment in Galatians?

> If you really fulfill the royal law according to the Scripture, "You shall love your neighbor as yourself," you do well. But if you show partiality, you commit sin and are convicted by the law as transgressors. For whoever keeps the whole law but fails in one point has become guilty of all of it. For he who said, "Do not commit adultery," also said, "Do not kill." If you do not commit adultery but do kill, you have become a transgressor of the law.
>
> So speak and act as those who are to be judged under the law of liberty. For judgment is without mercy to the one who has shown no mercy; yet mercy triumphs over judgment.
>
> [Jas 2:8–13]

An Early Christian Tradition: Love Fulfills the Law

Jas 5:19f provided a parallel for dealing with sinful Christians similar to that in Gal 6:1–3. This passage from James shows other parallels to the tradition of love as fulfillment of the law that we studied in Gal 5. Since it is unlikely that Paul is dependent on Jas, the existence of two parallel traditions suggests that Paul has not invented Gal 5 to deal with the Galatian situation. Rather, the basic pattern, "law of liberty," "love of neighbor fulfills the law," and even the concluding implication that "mercy" is what counts in the judgment, was probably a standard part of early Christian ethical teaching. Jas is almost entirely devoted to traditions with Hellenistic Jewish parallels. It seems probable that this tradition developed among such Jewish Christians. The community to which Jas is addressed may have been primarily a Jewish Christian one. Its language seems to be internally directed and has parallels with the sectarian language used by the Essenes [Ward, 1966:108; 1968:290]. The error envisaged in 5:19 is wandering from the community of the elect. The writing is concerned with relations between members of the community. This section is a commentary on two passages from Leviticus—19:18, on love of neighbor, and 19:15, against partiality. Perhaps this section was a set Jewish Christian interpretation of Lev. That section of the Scripture may have been called "royal law" in that Jewish Christian interpretation [Dibelius:142f].

Both "law of liberty" and "perfect law of freedom" in Jas 1:25 is a typical Hellenistic Jewish expression. It was used to distinguish Jews from Gentiles. Aristeas 31 uses it to indicate the perfection of the Jewish law. The king is told that he should obtain a translation of the Old Testament for his library because "the law it contains, inasmuch as it is of divine origin, is full of wisdom and free from all blemish." When it was combined with Stoic images of one cosmic law, obedience to the Jewish law could be seen as the culmination of the ethical ideal of free obedience to the law of the cosmos. James evidently saw the Christians as free from the Jewish interpretation of the law. He combines Jewish traditions of two-way paraenesis with the sayings of Jesus throughout the writing [Dibelius:116–20; 141–43]. This tradition shares with both Paul and the Synoptic tradition the combination of love command, decalogue, fulfillment of the law, and Christian freedom from the Jewish understanding of the law.

The concluding "mercy triumphs over judgment" assures the Christian that fulfillment of the love command is the standard for judgment [Mussner:124; Ward, 1966:78–108].

The Love Command Against Partiality in the Community

Jas picks up on partiality because it is the problem which afflicts his community. [Ward, 1969] Lev 19:15 makes partiality a sin against the love command. We have already seen that the love of neighbor was commonly paired with the decalogue, especially examples of adultery and murder [Sir 34:26; TGad 4:6f; Mussner:126; this pairing makes the comparison between murder and hating the brother in 1 Jn 3:15]. Jas argues that to violate the law of love by showing partiality is equivalent to violating the whole law. Paul makes a similar claim with regard to the ritual law in Gal 5:3. Verse 12 makes the warning implied in the passage quite specific: the Christian will be judged on the basis of the law of freedom. The contrast between saying and doing leads to other examples. Jas is frequently concerned with the contrast between what people say and what they do. Jas 2:14–17 presents Abraham as an example of "doing," works, and not just saying. He was considered blessed because of his hospitality in Jewish traditions, which Jas is apparently using [Ward:1968]. James is reprimanding wealthy Christians for their failure to show love/ mercy to the poor of the community.

Both the partiality shown rich members of the community (2:1–7) and the failure of the rich to aid the poor violate the basic principles for which that community stands. This behavior can hardly be based on the example of Abraham who showed hospitality to strangers [Ward, 1968:288–90].

The saying about judgment and mercy in v 13 seems to have been an independent saying, which Jas is using to link the two sections of the chapter together. Both Judaism and the Jesus tradition point out that divine judgment will face those without mercy (Sir 28:4; Prov 17:5; Tob 4:9–11; Mt 5:7; Mussner:127; Dibelius:147f). A variant of this tradition in TZeb 8:3 concludes its treatment of judgment according to the measure of love/mercy with "Mercy triumphs over judgment."

Thus, this section of Jas represents another version of the early Christian tradition that love of neighbor fulfills the law and wipes out the sins of the Christian. Jas is much closer to the Hellenistic Jewish origins of that tradition than either the Synoptic or the Pauline traditions, both of which have adapted it to communities made up of Gentile converts. But it would seem that Gentile converts were not the only ones to see in this tradition a way beyond the complexities of the legal obligations of the Jewish law. This view may have already been fostered in those sectors of Hellenistic Judaism which used summaries of the law in the double command or the double command plus the decalogue. Thus, Jas is able to preserve and use most of that ethical teaching without finding it in any way contradictory to fulfillment of the law in the community.

STUDY QUESTIONS

1. List the fundamental points of the early Christian tradition about love as fulfillment of the law.

2. How does James differ from Paul?

3. Why does James single out partiality as a prime example of violation of the love command?

4. What does the expression "Mercy triumphs over judgment" mean?

9
LOVE OF ENEMIES AS WITNESS

Rom 12:9–21; 1 Pt 3:8–12

Compare the two passages below. They reflect a common early Christian tradition. 1 Pt is more influenced by the language of Hellenistic ethics than Rom. List as many parallels between the two passages as you can.

Let love be genuine; hate what is evil, hold fast to what is good; love one another with brotherly affection; outdo one another in showing honor. Never flag in zeal, be aglow with the Spirit, serve the Lord. Rejoice in your hope, be patient in tribulations, be constant in prayer. Contribute to the needs of the saints, practice hospitality.

Bless those who persecute you; bless and do not curse them. Rejoice with those who rejoice, weep with those who weep. Live in harmony with one another; do not be haughty, but associate with the lowly; never be conceited. Repay no one evil for evil, but consider what is noble in the sight of all. If possible, so far as it depends on you, live peaceably with all. Beloved, never avenge yourselves, but leave it to the wrath of God, for it is written, "Vengeance is mine; I will repay, says the Lord."

No, "If your enemy is hungry, feed him; if he is thirsty, give him drink; for by so doing you will heap burning coals on his head." Do not be overcome by evil, but overcome evil with good.

[Rom 12:9–21]

Finally, all of you, have unity of spirit, sympathy, love of the brethren, a tender heart and a humble mind.

Do not return evil for evil or reviling for reviling; but, on the contrary, bless, for to this you have been called, that you may obtain a blessing, for

"He that would love life and see good days, let him keep his tongue from evil and his lips from speaking guile; let him turn away from evil and do right; let him seek peace and pursue it. For the eyes of the Lord are upon the righteous, and his ears are open to their prayer. But the face of the Lord is against those who do evil."

[1 Pt 3:8–12]

From Love of Neighbor to Love of Enemy

The only explicit citations of Lev 19:18 outside the Synoptic tradition are in Rom 13:9, Gal 5:14 and Jas 2:8 [Berger:121f]. The use of that command in Jas appears to give "neighbor" a sectarian interpretation, which limits it to members of the community. We have seen that Jewish traditions fluctuate between the limited sense of neighbor and the more open one, which understood neighbor to refer to anyone with whom one has dealings. In the early Christian tradition, the love of enemies command can fulfill the functions of that wider use of neighbor (cf. 1 Th 5:15; Rom 12:14,17–20). It appears from the examples in Rom 12 and 1 Pt 3 that it had become traditional in early Christian ethical preaching to combine the two forms of love command: love toward members of the community and love toward outsiders.

This double focus keeps the love command from becoming as inwardly focused as it appears to be in sectarian communities like that at Qumran [Göppelt:128–30]. This combination may have come from further elaboration of the sayings of Jesus. 1 Pt 1:15–19 reapplies sayings of Jesus in his argument that Gentiles are now called to be among the "holy people" of God. That application includes citation of Lev 11:44f: the holiness of the people mirrors that of God. Though much of the love language appears to be limited to members of the Christian community, that community is never entirely closed off. "Do good to all, especially to members of the household of faith" (Gal 6:10) seems to have been a fairly common attitude. It would probably have been quite difficult for Gentile Christians to isolate themselves from outsiders. Often such converts still had non-Christian family. Both 1 Cor and 1 Pt clearly assume that the Christians addressed may well have pagan wives, husbands, or masters.

The love command appears to have been felt as grounded in Scripture rather than as a unique invention of Jesus. But Rom and 1 Pt use Old Testament quotations to give authority to the command to love enemies (cp. Jas 1:18; Göppelt:132). 1 Pt 3:8–9 moves quickly from love of fellow Christians to love of enemy. As is the case in most of the parallel examples, non-retaliation is the primary form taken by love of enemy: "Do not return evil for evil." Compare the beatitude in 1 Pt 3:14a, "But even if you do suffer for righteousness' sake, you will be blessed," and Mt 5:10. [Göppelt:234f]

Some interpreters argue that "love of enemies" in contexts like that of 1 Pt 3:9–14 represents the pragmatism of the underdog. Christians who must make the best of positions of inferiority and dependence upon pagan patrons, husbands or masters will simply make the best of it by not retaliating (quite unlike the example of love of enemy in the good Samaritan). However, the suggestions in Hellenistic Jewish writings that non-retaliation has the positive function of converting the enemy into a friend or even a proselyte suggest a more "active" reason for the early Christian teaching on love. Further, the texts in question are quite capable of describing the more pragmatic relationship that the Christian simply has to endure: "subjection." They include advice to Christians that tells them to "be subject" to a variety of rulers, masters, etc. Therefore, it seems more likely that "love of enemies" was perceived as an important part of Christian witness. Unlike passive endurance, one hoped that the enemy would become a friend or perhaps even a fellow Christian [Piper:47].

An Early Christian Tradition on Love of Brethren and Enemies

Extensive topical parallels between Rom 12–13 and 1 Pt 2–3 suggest that there was an established pattern of early Christian ethical preaching which dealt with relationships that Christians faced. The differences in the sayings about non-retaliation, which were already proverbial in Judaism, suggest that the parallels are due to a common thematic arrangement in the preaching of the community and not to some literary dependence of one text on the other [Piper:5–18; Göppelt:225 tries to nail the formulation in 1 Pt to a combination of Lk 6:27f and wisdom traditions such as Prov 17:3; 24:29; cf. 20:22; 1 En 1,4]. Further, the section on love of enemy represents a special topic in early Christian preaching. It does not belong to the tables of social relationships and duties that early Christians took over from Hellenistic moral preaching and then elaborated to suit their own situation [see the general discussion of such tables in Göppelt:163–79]. Both examples show that Christians distinguished between duties that were binding in connection with the larger community, indicated by words like "submit" and "do good to," and those that applied between Christians, associated with love of brethren and service [Piper:132; Göppelt:177f]. The following chart indicates the topical parallels between the two traditions:

Duties to (submit):	Romans	1 Peter
state	13:1–7	2:13–17
masters	—	2:18–25
spouses	—	3:1–7
love		
brothers	12:9–13, 15f	3:8
	13:8–10	
enemies	12:14, 17–21	3:9–12
(hostile neighbors)		

The traditions on love exhibit even more striking parallels in wording, though Rom is closer to the Jewish traditions and 1 Pt closer to general Hellenistic preaching. The following chart suggests that a common arrangement of topics underlies these passages:

1 Peter 3:8–9	Romans 12:10, 14, 16f
8: have unity of spirit	16: live in harmony with one another
sympathy, a tender heart	15: rejoice with those who rejoice, weep with those who weep
a humble mind	16: do not be haughty but associate with the lowly
9: do not return evil for evil	17: repay no one evil for evil (1 Th 5:15)
but bless	14: bless those who persecute you, bless ... (cp. 1 Cor 4:12)

Further, the only use of the Old Testament in this section of Rom is in the sections on love of enemy and neighbor. Rom 12:17–20 is a catena of Old Testament allusions: 17b—Prov 3:4; 18—Ps 33:14(?); 19a—Lev 19:18; 19b—Dt 32:35. And the longest quotation in 1 Pt is Ps 34:12–16 [Piper:111f]. Paul may well have reworked Old Testament quotations that were traditional in such preaching into his catena. The extensive grounding that the command to love enemies receives in both instances suggests that this command may have been felt to be one of the most difficult in its tradition.

Evangelization and Love of Enemy

The combination of the two forms of the love command in this tradition is more than an accidental combination of sayings from the Jesus tradition. The combination itself may be tied to the community's concern for evangelization. Look carefully at the language used to describe the relationships between Christians; fellowship, harmony, and unity play an important role. Sampley's study of fellowship and "having the same mind" language in Paul has set such expressions into a sharper legal and sociological context. Paul apparently followed the model of a Roman *societas,* a group of partners, bound together by verbal agreement for a common goal. Usually such arrangements were commercial but the emphasis on such fellowship language in Philippians as well as the known fact that the Philippians contributed to Paul's support and received an assessment from him of his missionary venture suggests that he and they had such a relationship for the purpose of evangelization. Phil 2:1–5 describes the "same mind" which represents the legal requirement that members be agreed on the goal of their association as the mind of Christ, of humility and love. Thus, Paul's missionary *societas* was felt to differ from the commercial kind in that it was seen to be grounded in Christ [Sampley:60–68]. These passages suggest that such language and sentiments may have been more widespread among early Christian churches. The image presented is that of a group unified for the purpose of giving testimony.

Unity of purpose is required of such associations. As soon as the partners no longer agree on the goal, the association is dissolved. At the same time, such evangelistic concerns would naturally require teaching on how one responds to hostility. The saying about not repaying evil for evil seems to have had a history of use in reference to the persecution suffered by missionaries. Paul uses it to refer to the sufferings of the apostle in 1 Cor 4:12. The command retains its missionary formulation in Rom 12:14, 17–21. But it is likely that the sayings were interpreted as applied to the numerous day to day hostilities faced by Christians.

1 Pt clearly perceives the situation of enmity envisaged by the teaching on love of enemies to be the kind of day to day hostility that a Christian might run into in his/her transactions with neighbors. Such antagonism might result from nothing more than the fact of a person's being Christian and the suspicion of subversion that attached to that fact in the ancient world [Göppelt:159–62, who notes the parallel with Mt 5:16 as suggesting a general feeling of missionary obligation among early Christians; ibid:226; Piper:132]. 1 Pt 2:12 explicitly states that the good conduct of the Christian among the pagans is considered important for the conversion of the latter.

Some interpreters object to the tone of the non-retaliation statement in Rom 12:19f. The quotation from Prov 25:21f parallels its use among the Essenes (1 QS x,17–20; CD ix,2–3) and merely defers vengeance until God can do a better job [Stendahl, 1962]. Most exegetes see that view as laying too much weight on what was a traditional Old Testament citation and does not do justice to the conclusion in v 21 [Kaesemann:330; Schlier:382–84; Fitzmyer, *JBC*:326]. The implication of that verse is that the enemy may yet be converted, since "love" is to overcome the evil that is done [Piper:116f].

Thus it seems likely that this whole complex of tradition belongs to the community's reflection on its role in winning others to Christianity. We have already seen that Paul shifts to such a focus in 1 Cor 10. His use of the command to love the enemy in discussing the sufferings of the apostle in 1 Cor 4:12 shows that the command had an important place in that tradition. But both Rom and 1 Pt recognize that the command is not simply directed at those who are being supported to be full-time missionaries. It provides guidance in all the situations faced by the community. The evangelical concerns of both writings make it clear that the tradition from which this command came never considered it simply the pragmatic adaptation of an underdog. Rather, it is an essential part of the testimony which Christians are to give to the world.

STUDY QUESTIONS

1. How did early Christian ethical preaching come to combine the love of neighbor and the love of enemy?

2. Give two reasons why it is incorrect to say that the early Christian ethic of non-retaliation is simply the pragmatic strategy for survival of an underdog.

3. What is the authority behind the command to love enemies according to this early Christian preaching?

4. How are love of fellow Christians and love of enemy related to evangelization?

5. What forms of hostility did early Christians have to face?

10
LOVE OF ENEMIES AND SUBMISSION TO AUTHORITIES

Compare the following two sections from Rom and 1 Pt. What is their view of the role of political authorities? Why do they instruct Christians to submit to authorities?

Rom 13:1–7	**1 Pt 2:13–17**
Let every person be subject to the governing authorities. For there is no authority except from God and those that exist have been instituted by God. Therefore, he who resists will incur judgment. For rulers are not a terror to good conduct, but to bad. Would you have no fear of him who is in authority? Then do what is good, and you will receive his approval, for he is God's servant for your good. But if you do wrong, be afraid, for he does not bear the sword in vain; he is the servant of God to execute his wrath on the wrongdoer.	Be subject for the Lord's sake to every human institution, whether it be to the emperor as supreme, or to governors as sent by him to punish those who do wrong and to praise those who do right.
Therefore one must be subject not only to avoid God's wrath, but also for conscience' sake.	For it is God's will that by doing right you should put to silence the ignorance of foolish men. Live as free men, without using your freedom as a pretext for evil; but live as servants of God.

For this reason you also pay taxes to whom taxes are due, revenue to whom revenue is due, respect to whom respect is due, honor to whom honor is due.

Honor all men, love the brother-hood, honor the emperor.

The Role of Political Authority in Hellenistic Thought

While the Christian paraenetic tradition can trace obedience to political authority back to the saying about "taxes to Caesar" (Mk 12:14–17), the rationale for obedience in this tradition is derived from Hellenistic Jewish political thought. It enabled Jews to view all political rulers in a positive light, since their authority derives from God [Aristeas 187–300; Kaesemann:339; Göppelt:180f]. Much of the language in these passages derives from the traditions of political rhetoric. It represents the "official speech" of public documents and proclamations and has nothing to do with the merits of the particular person holding an office. We have a similar tradition of titles and ways of addressing important political figures that also have nothing to do with our attitudes toward the individual holder of the office, and, indeed, no longer are used in common speech outside such ceremonial occasions. Such ways of speaking fulfill the functions of language that we spoke about as "cohesive." The person who uses them is demonstrating a willingness to belong to that particular social group and its institutions. Any first century reader would recognize that Rom, from a more Jewish perspective, and 1 Pt, from the more common Hellenistic way of speaking, are both making statements of that type. Consequently, they would not find anything particularly striking about much of what is said in these passages. Rather, the use of such language could be seen to evoke a particular mood, to reinforce social sentiments. It tells the reader that the Christian is willing to belong to the larger society, and that he/she is not out to subvert the social order [Kaesemann:338].

Within the biblical tradition, there is an alternative view of political order. That order can be seen as the human attempt to usurp the place which rightfully belongs to God. In apocalypses like Daniel and Revelation, the political powers who have the faithful under their control and are involved in persecuting at least some of them are pictured as demonic beasts who will be vanquished by the final victory of God (read Rev 13 & 17, for example). One can hardly imagine the Christians, who must resist offering worship to the emperor in Rev, concurring with the "Honor the emperor" attitude of this tradition. But it may have been just such traditions of obedience that created such a crisis for Christians in those persecutions. Rev has to use every symbolic means at its disposal to make the satanic character of imperial policy clear. Of course, even in Rev the Christian can only resist by refusing to obey the command to show loyalty by an act of worship such as throwing grains of incense before the emperor's statue, swearing an oath by the emperor and the gods (often a required part of business and legal transactions), or pouring out a libation to the emperor (often done at banquets). But Rom and 1 Pt assume that the Christian will face occasional hostility and irrational persecution. But they do not deal with the situation in which the political authorities are felt to be actively opposed to the truth of Christianity as such. Nor, in fact, does the ceremonial rhetoric employed in these passages deal with the question of political authorities who do not praise the good and punish the evil, with the kind of corruption of justice that the Old Testament prophets often speak against. They simply presume the normal situation in which the Christian must live under a reasonably functioning system of government and assert that Christianity is not out to subvert that order as such.

Submission as Accommodation to Weakness

The apocalyptic tradition shows that those who are powerless to change the political and social situation under which they live may nevertheless create powerful symbols of its corruption and falseness. We have already seen that Hellenistic thought could understand "love of enemy" to mean the pragmatic submission to persons on whom one is dependent. Many people today regard this tradition as a classic expression of that view. They argue that in the long run it simply keeps those who are weak and oppressed in their place. This tradition is quite different from Jesus' saying about "taxes to Caesar," which was uttered in a situation of potential revolt and whose irony would have been clear enough to his audience. The "submit" approach of this tradition always leaves the presumption of right/ good with the political authorities.

Many twentieth century Christians find such passages particularly problematic. Christianity is no longer a minority group which must struggle for its life. When a powerful organization adopts such rhetoric, it may of itself engender a passivity that assents to oppression. Such passivity then destroys the biblical message of love of neighbor and justice for the weak. The biblical community is to be committed to those goals. Consequently, they argue, Christians today cannot allow such rhetoric to distract them from the need to work against oppression. Liberation of the weak and oppressed is the concrete demand made by "love of neighbor" [Davis:2–5;14f;51f].

If one understands the rhetoric of the tradition from which these passages come, one need not oppose them as violently as some liberation theologians do. Most of the distinctions that are made between "submit" and "love" correlate with situations in which the Christian could/could not reasonably be expected to take some action. We have seen that "love of neighbor" within the Christian community itself required a constant struggle against social divisions. The use of that tradition to counter Christian distinctions between rich and poor in Jas is instructive. Certainly, Christians can extend that sense of neighbor when they are in the position to do so. None of the New Testament traditions suggest that the emperor or imperial political order itself is the ideal image of what God intended human relationships to be. That ideal can only be partially recognized in the Christian community itself—"partially," because even the Christian community does not possess the full salvation and victory over evil that is associated with the end of the world. Nevertheless, these

Christian communities do have a real impetus to change their patterns of human relationship, the grace and presence of God himself. This motivation forms an important side to Christian conviction about change and its necessity that can hardly be duplicated by secular commitments to change born out of social theory. The biblical tradition insists that God mandates love and justice; it does not need to call people to a reasoned conviction of that necessity. The biblical tradition also recognizes that humans would not persevere in such efforts without "grace" [Davis:26f, 102f]. Further, recognition that all human efforts are "partial" reminds Christians that they cannot identify the rule of God with the necessarily incomplete attempts to realize that rule in human communities. We have already seen that Christians had to deal with failures of love in their own communities. They suggest a need to continued "exhortation" of one another as the key to preserving their ideals in such a situation [Schillebeeckx:745f].

The Eschatological Perspective

The eschatological perspective reduces human institutions to a provisional status, which is not denied even by the traditions of submission represented in these passages. The ideology against which Rev struggles is one which divinizes the emperor and renders the political order of which he is the symbolic embodiment absolute. Neither of these passages does that. They both make the ultimate source and judge of authority God himself. Consequently, to tell the Christian to submit because it is the will of God is not quite the same thing as the obedience to the emperor mandated in the ideology of the state. The Christian is obeying his God, not the gods of the emperor. The "order and peace" implied by such advice stands over against the possibility that "Christian freedom" might imply disregard for the larger social order. 1 Pt makes it clear that Christians are "free" and only obey out of that freedom. Both passages see Christian obedience as motivated by a commitment to God which is quite beyond the fear of punishment if they are caught doing evil. Such active use of one's freedom is not the personally demeaning position of a weak underdog [Göppelt:186–88; Fitzmyer, *JBC:*123]. The Christian pays what is due out of conscience, not fear (Rom 13:1–7). The Christian must use his freedom in such a way that he silences any possible slander (1 Pt 2:15). Thus, anyone who might bring a case against him must be making a false accusation (1 Pt 4:15). That consideration itself shows how far this advice is from a passive, let government be, approach. The Christian will have false charges against which he/she has to fight. Providing people with real evils done by Christians could destroy the entire movement. It could even make it more difficult for others to defend themselves against false charges. Thus, the early Christian communities had an important stake in making it clear that they were not subverting the larger community. They had an important stake in the conduct of their members.

The eschatological perspective also makes an important difference to our understanding of the "feeling tone" of Christian freedom. We have already suggested that this "freedom" guarded the dignity of all members of the community. "Submission" is never a statement of the relative worth of individuals. Christians fought against the persistent efforts to introduce the hierarchical structures and value judgments of the larger society into their own communities. Contrary to common opinion, a person's standing in the social hierarchy was never an indication of that person's worth or even status in the eyes of the divine. The preaching of Cynic/Stoic philosophers also opposed the freedom of the philosopher to such social conventions. But the tone of that opposition as well as the reasoning which supported it differs from the "eschatological freedom" of the Christian. The Stoic wise man follows the law of the cosmos. Free from the passions and concerns of other people, he accepts whatever happens to him, since such events are not under his control. His reactions to those events, which are under the control of his reason, keep him from the distress they cause others. Christian freedom is quite different from this Stoic self-control and passionlessness. The victory of salvation is anticipated in the gift of the Spirit. That gift also leads the Christian to proclaim a freedom from the powers of the universe, not resignation to their operation (1 Pt 1:18; Göppelt:187f). Of course, it is a freedom grounded in the sovereignty of God, not in human action. Nevertheless, it carries an important message for the believer. He/she may "submit" to political authorities, but he/she is not ultimately subject to enslavement by them or by any other powers which might claim to control the world. The use of common political language in these passages should not be allowed to obscure the other structures of Christian experience which give them a quite different ring.

STUDY QUESTIONS

1. What type of language is being used in the passages about submission to authorities? Give a modern example of such language.

2. How does Christian obedience to such authority differ from that attributed to other members of society?

3. What other view(s) of political authority are contained in the Bible?

4. What situation does each view of political authority in the Bible address?

5. Why are many twentieth century Christians concerned with liberation and justice? How does the Christian approach to such questions differ from one based simply on political concerns?

6. Why is the "eschatological perspective" of Christian obedience important?

11
GOD AS LOVE: THE JOHANNINE TRADITION

Jn 13–17; 1 Jn

We will be studying passages from Jn 13–17 and 1 Jn. Read them through as a whole. See how many of the special characteristics of the Johannine tradition you can pick out in those writings.

Special Characteristics of the Johannine Tradition

Recent Johannine scholarship has focused on the relationship between the special characteristics of the Johannine writings and the history of that community's development [Brown, 1979]. Many of those characteristics are evident in the passages which deal with love. Some of them have raised questions about the extent to which Johannine Christians extended love to those outside their own community, particularly toward the Jewish authorities who were hostile to the community (cf. Jn 16:1–4a).

1. Hellenistic Jewish wisdom traditions played an important role in the development of Johannine thought. They enabled Johannine Christians to picture Jesus as the divine Word. They also influenced Johannine interpretation of the love command [Berger:173]. The passages in which the love command appears in John's Gospel all come from the farewell discourses, which contain Jesus' final instructions to his disciples. In the Hellenistic Jewish traditions of the love command, we found the closest parallels to the double com-

mand, love of God and neighbor, in the "testament" genre, that is, in writings or sections of writings which contained the final instructions of an Old Testament patriarch to his sons. Like those patriarchs, Jesus exhorts his disciples to unity and love [Berger:121; Brown II:599f]. John sees love within the community as a manifestation of God/Jesus dwelling with the community (14:23). TJos promises that God will dwell with those who keep his commandments (x,2; xi,1).

2. Johannine thought takes all metaphors and symbols of salvation and unifies them in Jesus. He is the one about whom all symbols speak. This unification makes it clear that Jesus is greater than any other means of salvation [MacRae, 1970]. Similarly, the teaching of Jesus is unified in the single commandment of love. The supreme example of love is found in the identity of Jesus and the Father. Thus, the Johannine tradition provides a new theistic grounding for the love command: it is rooted in God's love for the world, which is manifested in the mission of Jesus [e.g., Jn 3:16–21; Brown I:142; Perkins, 1978:45–47; Schnackenburg I:398–408]. The Johannine unification of love language makes it the foundation of the community. The transcendent reality of God, the love between Father and Son, is revealed in and through the life of the Christian community and its expression of love.

3. The Johannine community appears to be very inwardly directed. Apocalyptic symbolism is used to reinforce loyalty to that community over against those outside, "the world," darkness, those whose hostility to Jesus is reflected in their hostility to the community. In this picture, hostility to Jesus is equivalently hostility to God. Consequently, the Fourth Gospel speaks in the most negative way against Jesus' Jewish opponents. They become murderers and children of Satan (Jn 8). Those who fail to recognize the Father and Jesus are objects of God's own hatred [16:2f; Schillebeeckx:406]. Of course, persecution suffered by the community at the hands of the Jews seems to have cost it members and provoked this intense turn toward solidarity, love of fellow members of the community and the like. But it seems to have almost erased the tradition of love of ene-

my. The same symbolism which had been formulated to protect the community against the inroads made by Jewish opposition is turned against dissident members of the Johannine tradition in 1 Jn. That turn points to the dangers of such dualistic symbolization. It may intensify opposition and make reconciliation difficult if not impossible. It appears to justify hating others, Jews or dissident Christians in the name of God [Brown, 179:131–35].

However, several qualifications should be introduced into this negative picture. Presentation of one's opponents in demonic symbols was common among minority groups of the period. One should, perhaps, be more struck by the fact that the realized eschatology of the Johannine tradition left Christians without the imaginative outlet of fantasizing all the torments that the judgment might inflict on their opponents. Further, the Johannine community was never in a position to act upon such symbols. They could never harm their opponents "in the name of God." Even the elder in 2 and 3 Jn has only the authority of persuasion. He can suggest that churches not receive the dissident Christians but he cannot force that issue. (3 Jn shows that his own emissaries met with the same sort of hostility.) Despite the inner-directedness of the Johannine love language, the community never became an isolated, perfectionist sect like that at Qumran [Bogart]. The foundation of its fellowship in the divine commission to continue the witness of his Son [Schnackenburg, 1970:66–72] kept the community oriented toward the world. Evangelization is still a primary task of the Johannine community. Finally, recognition that the immanent presence of God is the real foundation of Christian community requires a certain acknowledgement of the limits of human actions in the face of the all-encompassing mystery [Schillebeeckx:68].

The Love Command as the Testament of Jesus

The Fourth Gospel presents the love command as the testament of Jesus. As such, both love of fellow Christian and love of enemy are involved. The farewell discourses present the love command as the basis of three relationships: (A) it defines relationships between members of the community; (B) those relationships in turn are founded on the special relationship of presence that the community enjoys with God/Jesus and Spirit; (C) it must also be reflected in Jesus' commissioning his followers to represent him before a hostile world.

> A new commandment I give to you that you love one another; even as I have loved you, you must also love one another. By this all will know that you are my disciples, if you have love for one another.
>
> [Jn 13:34f]

A. The farewell discourses begin by making love between Christians the commandment (cf. 1 Jn 2:7; 3:11, 23). Though the formulation directs that love toward members of the community, the expectation that it will be recognized by outsiders indicates that it has a tie to the evangelization expected of the community. The command is clearly grounded in the example of Jesus (cp. 15:12; and even in the example of God, 3:16). Since it is the only commandment in the Johannine tradition of ethical preaching as we have it recorded, we no longer find it as summary or fulfillment of the law. Rather the love command bears all the weight of Christian ethical obligation [Perkins:152–55; Brown II:612–14].

> "If you love me you will keep my commandments." Judas (not Iscariot) said to him, "Lord, how is it that you will manifest yourself to us?" Jesus answered him, "If a man loves me, he will keep my word, and my Father will love him, and we will come to him and make our home with him. He who does not love me does not keep my words; and the word which you hear is not mine but the Father's who sent me."
>
> [Jn 14:15,22–24]

B. This section presents us with the combination that "loving Jesus" means keeping his commandments. Some exegetes think that it represents the Johannine tradition's version of the double love command with love of Jesus replacing love of God. The connection between keeping the commandments and a special presence of God with his people was made in Hellenistic Judaism as we have seen. This passage shows that the Johannine community sees that eschatological presence of God realized in itself.

Verses 22–24 answer a possible objection to such an eschatological claim: Jesus did not return to the world in the visible way expected by messianic texts both Jewish and Christian. The Johannine tradition has taken the emphasis off such future eschatology. Indeed, Jesus does not return to the world. It has already shown by its hostility that it does not love him or keep his commandments. Instead, Jesus returns only to the community of those who do keep his word, which is the word of God [Perkins:162–66; Schnackenburg III:91f]. The combination of a variety of indwelling sayings in this section of the discourse makes the community the dwelling place of God, e.g. vv 16f, the Spirit/Paraclete; vv 18, 21, Jesus manifesting himself to the one who loves him; v 23, Jesus and the Father love and dwell with the one who keeps Jesus' word. Thus, the community fulfills the promise that the time of worship "in spirit and truth" is coming (4:21–24; Brown II:647f). This divine presence in the community is the real defense of the truth of Jesus' teaching against all who attack it. It ties the fate of the community to that of Jesus, since just as Jesus is the unique source of salvation, the community is the unique presence of that salvation.

> If you abide in me, and my words abide in you, ask whatever you will, and it shall be done for you.
> By this is my Father glorified, that you bear much fruit and so prove to be my disciples.
> As the Father has loved me, so have I loved you; abide in my love. If you keep my commandments, you will abide

in my love, just as I have kept my Father's commandments and abide in his love.

These things I have spoken to you that my joy may be in you, and that your joy may be full.

This is my commandment, that you love one another as I have loved you. Greater love has no man than this, that a man lay down his life for his friends. You are my friends if you do what I command you. No longer do I call you servants, for a servant does not know what his master is doing; but I have called you friends, for all that I have heard from the Father, I have made known to you. You did not choose me, but I chose you and appointed you that you should go and bear fruit and that your fruit should abide; so that whatever you ask the Father in my name, he may give it to you.

This I command you, to love one another.

[Jn 15:7–17]

C. This commentary on the vine image of vv 1–6 opens up several dimensions of the role played by the love command in the Johannine community [Brown II:665–83]. The "abiding" language in Jn always means to be a disciple of Jesus. Consequently, the passage encourages Christians not to give up under persecution (v 18). But "abiding" is not simply concerned with remaining in the community. Christians must glorify God by "bearing much fruit," apparently a reference to the fact that they will have to witness to Jesus before the hostile world (cf. 15:27). Thus, the community is being entrusted with continuing Jesus' own mission.

The Pauline emphasis on the *imitatio Christi* in the life of the suffering apostle finds its Johannine counterpart here as well. The obedience of the community to Jesus' commandments is equivalent to Jesus' perfect obedience to the Father. Though this section mentions commandments in the plural, the only commandment ever stated is the love commandment (similarly elsewhere in the Johannine tradition). The highest example and foundation of that love is Jesus' death for his friends, for—unlike the Pauline use of servant/slave metaphors—the Johannine disciples are now friends, not slaves.

The introduction of friendship makes it possible to expand the love commandment with themes from the Hellenistic friendship tradition. True friendship was commonly said to be between those equal in virtue. Jewish traditions applied this ideal to Moses, the friend of God. Here Jn has expanded that friendship to include all who are united with Jesus/the Father. The wisdom tradition also held that the righteous are "friends of God" (Wis 7:27). One of the privileges of such a friend of God, which was particularly exemplified in Moses, was that such a person could speak boldly (in prayer) to God. This privilege of prayer is also being extended to the disciples. Jesus as the incarnate divine wisdom now extends to his disciples a privilege that had been thought to belong only to a few righteous ones. They are now friends of God [Schnackenburg III:125f]. However, Jn makes it clear that this new status does not derive from the particular progress toward philosophic virtue which Jewish tradition attributed to Moses. Christians are "friends of God" because they are "friends of Jesus." That friendship is grounded, not in equality of virtue, but in the Christian community's obedience to his command of love [Perkins:174–76].

However, one should not think that the community meets the obligations of this friendship simply by fostering mutual love between its members [pace Schnackenburg III:127f]. It has the obligation to "bear fruit," to bear witness before the world. Indeed, for Jn Jesus' mission is only complete when he leaves this group of disciple-friends to continue his witness in the world.

> The glory which thou hast given me, I have given them, that they may be one even as we are one, I in them, and thou in me, that they may become perfectly one, so that the world may know that thou hast sent me and hast loved them even as thou hast loved me.

Father, I desire that they also whom thou hast given
me, may be with me where I am, to behold my glory which
thou hast given me in thy love before the foundation of the
world.

O righteous Father, the world has not known Thee,
but I have known Thee; and these know that Thou hast
sent me. I made known to them Thy name, and I will make
it known, that the love with which Thou hast loved me
may be in them and I in them.

[Jn 17:22–26]

D. Jn 17 presents Jesus' prayer commissioning the disciples.
The eschatological presence of God with the community is expressed
in images of divine glory and unity (the latter was important among
the Essenes; cp. 1 QS v,2,7). Now, in line with the theistic unification
of Johannine symbols, both belong to that special relationship Jesus
has with the Father. They are "transferred" to the community, since
that community knows God/Jesus and will now have to testify to
that truth in the world which does not know God [Perkins,
1978:203–206]. Once again, we find that the love which typifies
members of this new community is much more than a relationship
between human persons. It reflects the essence of the relationship between the Father and Jesus [Schnackenburg III:225]. Since its life in
the world reflects the relationship between God and Jesus as it has
been manifested through Jesus, the community may also expect to
share the glory that Jesus has with God in the future. This reserva-
tion makes it clear that the glory of God's presence in the community is not the fullness of divine glory. Jn 15 pointed out that these
disciples were only "friends of God" through Jesus' choice of them,
not through any merits of their own. Now we learn that that choice,
as with everything Jesus does, was a gift to him from the Father.
Once again all the Johannine symbols are drawn together into the
unity between Jesus and the Father.

Love in a Fractured Community: 1 Jn

With 1 Jn, we get to read another page in the life of the Johannine community. We can see how the extraordinary symbolism and insight of the evangelist was transmitted by one of his disciples after his death. After the striking picture of divine unity as the foundation of the community drawn in the Gospel of Jn, and the importance of that unity/love as the witness the community bears before the world, one can sense the traumatic shock of the events reflected in 1 Jn. The fellowship has been split. A dissident group of Christians, with some following, has formed. Perhaps, their departure was facilitated by the death of the evangelist (an explanation of which was inserted into the Gospel, 21:23). The author of 1 Jn is encouraging Johannine Christians to remain in fellowship with him. They must do so, he claims, if they are going to stand with the tradition which they have had from the beginning. The division between the two groups of Johannine Christians seems to have been over theological points. However, it is very difficult to reconstruct what those points were because much of 1 Jn is polemical rhetoric and does not contain an account of the opposing views. At the very least, the dissident group seems to have denied that Jesus' death was an atonement for sin, and to have required that Christians achieve a high state of ethical perfection if they are to be saved (1:8 hints that they may have claimed to have attained that state themselves; Brown 1979:123–32).

We do not have to concern ourselves with reconstructing the points under dispute. Much of 1 Jn is not aimed at theological debate with dissidents. Rather, the author is repeating the common traditions of Johannine preaching, what the Johannine Christians have heard "since the beginning." This repetition founds the author's claim that fellowship with him represents the true Johannine community and hence the true fellowship with God [Schnackenburg, 1970:2; Perkins, 1979:22]. Naturally, the love command continues to be the command which is the basis of the community and of salvation. According to the author, the dissidents have violated that love.

And by this we may be sure that we know him, if we keep his commandments. He who says, "I know him," but disobeys his commandments is a liar, and the truth is not in him; but whoever keeps his word, in him, truly, love of God is perfected. By this we may be sure that we are in him: he who says he abides in him ought to walk in the same way in which he walked.

Beloved, I am writing you no new commandment, but an old commandment, which you had from the beginning; the old commandment is the word which you have heard. Yet I am writing you a new commandment, which is true in him and in you, because the darkness is passing away and the true light is already shining. He who says he is in the light and hates his brother is in the darkness still. He who loves his brother abides in the light and in it there is no cause for stumbling. But he who hates his brother is in the darkness and walks in the darkness, and does not know where he is going because the darkness has blinded his eyes.

[1 Jn 2:3–11]

A. This section of exhortation may have been derived from the tradition of baptismal preaching in the Johannine community. Once again, the entire ethical instruction of the Christian is focused on the love commandment. Much of the language of this passage reminds us of the Fourth Gospel, e.g. "abiding in him," "keeping his commandments," "love of God perfected in one who keeps his commandments." This passage also employs the distinction between saying and doing, which is common in such ethical preaching and which we met in Jas. The general ethical exhortation of the Johannine community may have included specific examples such as we find in the next section.

For this is the message which you have heard from the beginning: we should love one another and not be like Cain who was of the Evil One and murdered his brother. And why did he murder him? Because his own deeds were evil and his brother's were righteous. Do not wonder, brethren, that the world hates you. We know that we have passed out of death into life, because we love the brethren. He who does not love the brethren remains in death. Anyone who hates his brother is a murderer and you know that no murderer has eternal life abiding in him.

By this we know love, that he laid down his life for us; and we ought to lay down our lives for the brethren. But if anyone has the world's goods and sees his brother in need, yet closes his heart against him, how does God's love abide in him? Little children, let us not love in word or speech, but in deed and truth.

[1 Jn 3:11–18]

B. This section shows how other themes of early Christian ethical preaching were integrated into the Johannine focus on the love command. We saw in Jas that the love command was connected with the decalogue prohibition of murder. In the same section Jas uses the word/deed contrast and points to the need to aid the poor members of the community: "If a brother or sister is ill-clad and in lack of daily food, and one of you says to them, 'Go in peace, be warmed and filled,' without giving them the things needed for the body, what does it profit? So faith without works is dead" (2:15–17). The Jas parallel shows that 1 Jn has combined traditional Christian themes. The targumic tradition held that Abel's sacrifice was accepted because of his righteousness, and Cain's rejected for unrighteousness. 1 Jn has employed that tradition here. At the same time, the intensification of the love imagery makes "hatred of the brethren" equivalent to murder. This equation can be seen as a transformation of the traditional "Violation of one command is a violation of all," which Jas used to argue that the lack of love manifested in partiality within the community was as serious as murder or adultery.

1 Jn has expanded this traditional pattern with the Johannine

image of the death of Christ as the prime example of love (cf. Jn 15:13). The community is ultimately based on that act of love. While Jas had love of the brethren manifested in charity as the work which proves a person's faith, 1 Jn has the same theme in its Johannine version. The Christians know that they have eternal life by the love for the brethren. That love should extend as far as Jesus' did in laying down his life for his friends. The practical demand which follows that reminder comes as something of a relief, since it is rendered less difficult by contrast. A Christian who has the ability to do so must not close his/her heart to the needs of the poor of the community.

This general instruction also has a polemic edge. Christians are reminded that they must expect hatred from the world. However, they can be sure that anyone who practices such "hatred" does not have eternal life. 1 Jn may have the dissident Christians in view when he makes such remarks, though the original argument over who possessed salvation/eternal life seems to have been formulated prior to the writing of the Gospel, when Johannine Christians were defending their claims against Jewish objections. That conflict was the original source of "hatred by the world" language as we have seen. Thus, this whole section is, as the author claims, an example of what the Johannine tradition has been "from the beginning." It shows us how "love of the brethren" brought traditional themes of early Christian ethical preaching together to define the meaning of righteousness for the community. [Schnackenburg, 1970:194–98;Perkins, 1979:44–46].

> By this we know that we are of the truth and reassure our hearts before him whenever our hearts condemn us, for God is greater than our hearts, and he knows everything. Beloved, if our hearts do not condemn us, we have confidence before God; and we receive from him whatever we ask, because we keep his commandments and do what pleases him. And this is his commandment, that we believe in the name of his Son Jesus Christ and love one another just as he commanded us.

All who keep his commandments abide in him, and he in them. And by this we know that he abides in us, by the Spirit which he has given us.

[1 Jn 3:19–24]

C. This section begins with a theme which we have met elsewhere in early Christian preaching such as the slogan in 1 Cor 8:3: the Christian can be confident in the judgment even if his/her heart (1 Cor, "conscience") might condemn, for God is greater. In order to appreciate the ubiquity of this problem, we must constantly remind ouselves that the communities of the ancient world in which Christians had to make their way were all like "small towns." Everyone knew everyone, and social pressure to conform to the standards of the community was much higher than anything twentieth century Americans experience. Insofar as he/she had to depart from those traditions, the Christian was forced into a crisis of "conscience," since conscience had been formed according to the norms of the society in which the Christian had been brought up—not those of the faith to which he/she has converted. In the case of the Johannine community, the problem of conscience seems to have been intensified by the perfectionism of the dissident Christians. The author reminds his readers of the tradition, well-known to them and us from the Gospel, that Jesus/Spirit abide with those who keep the commandment of love. Consequently, the real source of perfection in the Christian community is the divine presence, not the details of individual behavior. We have already seen in the Gospel that the double love command in the Johannine tradition appears to have been: "Love Jesus and the brethren." Verse 23 provides explicit evidence for that interpretation, since it presents "Believe in Jesus and love one another" as the command from God, which has been given the Johannine community as the basis of salvation by Jesus. That double command was probably also formulated in the struggles with Judaism prior to the writing of the Gospel. At that time, it served to remind Christians to stick with their faith in Jesus as Son of God and remain in the Christian community [Schnackenburg, 1970:201–208; Perkins, 1979:46–48]. The author of 1 Jn is using what the community already knows to address a new crisis over salvation. Remain with those who "believe in Jesus and love one another" and the presence of the Spirit abiding in that community assures one of salvation.

> Beloved, let us love one another; for love is of God, and he who loves is born of God and knows God. He who does not love does not know God; for God is love.
>
> In this, the love of God was made manifest among us, that God sent his only Son into the world, so that we might live through him. In this is love, not that we loved God but that he loved us and sent his Son to be the expiation for our sins.
>
> Beloved, if God so loved us, we also ought to love one another. No man has ever seen God; if we love one another, God abides in us and his love is perfected in us. By this, we know that we abide in him and he in us, because he has given us of his own Spirit. And we have seen and testify that the Father has sent his Son as the Savior of the world. Whoever confesses that Jesus is the Son of God, God abides in him, and he in God. So we know and believe the love that God has for us.
>
> God is love, and he who abides in love, abides in God, and God abides in him. In this is love perfected with us, that we may have confidence in the day of judgment, because as he is so are we in this world.
>
> There is no fear in love, but perfect love casts out fear. For fear has to do with punishment, and he who fears is not perfected in love. We love because he first loved us. If anyone says, "I love God," and hates his brother, he is a liar; for he who does not love the brother he has seen cannot love God, whom he has not seen.
>
> And this is the commandment we have from him, that he who loves God should love his brother also.

D. This passage brings together all of the themes associated with the Johannine teaching on love. It shows how that one command became the focal point for Johannine soteriology, Johannine christology and Johannine ethics. Further, it shows that the ultimate source of this teaching on love is the nature of God himself: "God is love." This insight makes it clear that the love command itself is not to be considered a human achievement. It is not to be considered simply as the highest ethical insight of a rational humanism, for example. Rather, it is a religious insight into the very essence of God himself. And it has only, according to the Johannine tradition, been shown to be such in the sending of the Son as Savior of humanity. Consequently, 1 Jn insists that believing in Jesus is necessary to true knowledge of God. Further, the Christian obligation to love is grounded in the love of God received. Once again, a theme which has been implicit in many of the treatments of the love command is presented in the Johannine symbolism at its most radical level. The love which is to be perfected in the Christian community is the love which belongs to the essence of God himself [Schnackenburg, 1970:233–35].

Throughout the treatment of the love command, we have seen that it assured Christians that they need not "fear" judgment. Even in their obedience to political authorities, Christians are to act out of conscience and obedience to God rather than fear of punishment. Again, the Johannine tradition has transformed that theme through its reflection on the love command. There is no room for fear in the love of God which is perfected in love of one another [Perkins, 1979:53–57]. However, the references to testimony to what the Christian knows and to the necessity that a person come to "confess" Jesus as Savior remind us that internally directed love is not the only obligation of the Johannine community. They are "as he is in the world." God abides with those who testify to the faith that the "Father has sent his Son as Savior of the world." This community never forgets its obligation to witness to Jesus in the world.

The section concludes with another Johannine version of the

double love command [Houlden, 1973:120f; Berger:166]. Love of God cannot exist without love of brother.

> Everyone who believes that Jesus is the Christ is a child of God, and everyone who loves the parent loves the child. By this we know that we love the children of God: when we love God and obey his commandments. For this is the love of God, that we keep his commandments. And his commandments are not burdensome.
>
> [1Jn 5:1–3]

E. The final section on the love command repeats the theme of 1 Jn 4:20f. It begins with what must have been a common proverb, "He who loves the parent loves the child," and applies that proverb somewhat awkwardly to the double love command. The concluding "His commandments are not burdensome" may be an allusion to the Jesus tradition as it was preserved in the Johannine community. Mt 11:28–30 preserves a wisdom saying, which originally spoke of the "lightness" of the yoke of wisdom (Sir 51:23–26). In Mt, Jesus speaks as divine wisdom promising that "my yoke is easy and my burden light." 1 Jn appears to represent a tradition which had applied that saying to the love command as the summary of all Christian obligation. Once again, that application was probably forged in the controversies with Judaism. 1 Jn reminds his readers that it is at the base of their tradition.

What Happened to "Love of Enemies"?

Commentators cannot help but be troubled by the seeming disparity in the Johannine reflection on love. On the one hand, it would not be possible to find a more profound statement of the depth of meaning in the double love command when seen in light of the death of Jesus as the revelation of God's love for humanity. On the other hand, the Johannine community seems to be rooted in hostility toward outsiders. 2 Jn 10 even directs that the dissident Christians be excluded from the hospitality of Johannine churches. As one of my students protested, "Isn't he just turning around and doing the same thing he condemns in others?" There is no simple answer to his question. We are in the dark about the extent of the controversy that was going on in the Johannine community and must be very cautious about evaluating such brief passages.

Although we never meet "love of enemies" as a theme in Johannine preaching, there are suggestions of a somewhat more universal scope to the love of the Johannine community. The formulation of the double command in 1 Jn 4:21, for example, appears to retain the connotations of the neighbor as anyone with whom one has dealings [so Schnackenburg, 1970:121f]. The image of the nature of God himself as love is quite unique in the Johannine milieu. We do not find any close parallels to it [Schnackenburg, 1970:231–37]. The Johannine writings clearly recognize that divine love is directed toward the salvation of the whole world (Jn 3:16; 1 Jn 4:9f, 14). Since the community itself exists to bear witness to that salvation in the world, it cannot simply reject outsiders. Indeed, evangelization is one of the expressions of the divine love present with the community that is called to be "as he is in the world."

These observations do not remove all difficulties with the negative language and dualism of the Johannine tradition. We may try to understand that in terms of the hostility faced by the community. We have already seen that the Christian evaluation of political authority can be positive in the usual circumstances of daily life envisaged by Rom and 1 Pt, and yet turn to the most negative, satanic symbolism when faced with the crisis of persecution and claims of imperial divinity in Rev. Similarly, we must suppose that the crisis faced by the Johannine tradition was more serious that we might suppose from the few references to Jewish persecution in the Gospel or to the dissidents in 1 Jn. Both crises have "exclusion" as a common problem. The Gospel refers to the crisis created when the Jews excluded Christians from the synagogue. Such a ban would ordinarily mean that members of the synagogue would have no dealings with the excluded Christians. Yet, people could not just "up and move" as they might in North America. Consequently, you can see that the ban would have all sorts of negative effects on a person's life; family, friends, and business might all be seriously affected. In the second crisis, the dissident Christians have withdrawn from fellowship with the author's community. The elder sees that withdrawal as "hatred of the brethren" equivalent to that earlier experience of excommunication by the Jews, since it rips apart the unity of the community, which, as we saw in Jn 17, was to be founded in the unity of Father and Son.

However understandable the intense situations which generated the Johannine rhetoric may be, one must also agree with Brown [1979:132–36] that the dualistic language adopted could easily undermine the fabric of love, which the Johannine tradition perceives as the essence of the Christian vision. Though the severity of these crises made it difficult for Johannine Christians to symbolize their relationship to the world in positive terms, one would expect that in less severe situations God's love for the world might be more fully and positively expressed. After all, no matter how hostile the world, Christians must still remain in that world to testify to the truth of God's saving love in Jesus.

STUDY QUESTIONS

1. Give three special characteristics of the Johannine tradition along with an example of each one from the Gospel or 1 Jn.

2. Give two examples of Johannine use of proverbial or wisdom traditions.

3. Give two examples of Johannine interpretation of typical themes in early Christian ethical preaching.

4. What are the "negative characteristics" of Johannine symbolism? How should we understand them?

5. How does the Johannine tradition use love to unify its image of God, of Jesus, of salvation, of the nature of the Christian community and of ethical obligation?

6. Give a brief description of the crises which faced the Johannine community. What response to those crises do we find in the Johannine writings?

7. How does the Johannine tradition understand the Christian obligation to "witness to the truth"?

EPILOGUE

Some Applications For Today

Jesus' metaphors and parables suggested that love of neighbor/enemy was the key to the nature of God. The Johannine tradition brought that insight to full expression. This divine love is the foundation and calling of the Christian community. Christians acknowledge that the love of neighbor/enemy is not a human achievement but flows from the love revealed in salvation and is revealed in the life and death of Jesus. We have seen that the traditions of early Christian ethical teaching brought these insights to bear on a number of issues facing their communities. We can hardly embark on formulating a "Christian ethic" for the twentieth century. The New Testament examples suggest that such an attempt would hardly be appropriate, since they recognize the real ethical task as formulating the insights of the tradition for the specific, differing circumstances of each community. Instead, we will suggest a few of the implications of this teaching with the hope that they will provoke you to ask your own questions about the ethical tasks facing the Christian Church.

1. The Christian is clearly obligated to seek solutions which promote good and avoid evil. The example of Jesus' death suggests that there is no point at which one can say "enough," "only so far" or "we will only promote this good if it doesn't interfere with our lives."

2. The "love" which is revealed as the essence of God is not a principle that can be demonstrated logically. It follows from a gratuitous act of salvation on God's part. Revelation of God's love for the world also requires a critique of the imperfect forms of human love.

Christians must look critically at all structures which enslave people. That criticism will include any claims to liberate one group at the expense of others. It recognizes the ambiguity inherent in human attempts to create salvation [Schillebeeckx:778f, 839].

3. The image of the Crucified as the key to divine love and liberation implies that no persons, not even the wicked, are outside that love. It implies that no persons can be sacrificed in the name of some project of liberation [Schillebeeckx:837f].

4. The image of God crucified shows a God suffering the evil and ambiguity of life along with humans. The New Testament does not present an "answer" to the problem of human suffering. It shows the perfection of a God who can "stand with" his suffering creation [Küng:694f].

5. Christian ethical reflection always remains an unfinished project much as our efforts of discipleship remain unfinished. The forgiveness of God and the presence of his rule do not require a utopian perfectionism of the Christian community [Piper:97f]. The disciple realizes that he/she continues to be an obedient servant in God's new creation as long as the present world continues. The present world is not negated by the new presence of salvation. That recognition also allows Christians to adopt—with revisions where necessary—whatever sources of ethical reflection are available in their cultural milieu. Christianity does not come with a pre-set legal, ethical, and social structure that is to be built on any site. It develops through dialogue between its founding insights and the situations in which Christians must witness [Piper:96].

6. Christians need not claim that they are the only religion which has any insight into love and compassion. Nevertheless, it is becoming increasingly evident that some religious vision is necessary to maintain those values in the modern world. The early Christians did not feel compelled to exalt the uniqueness of their ethical insights, but they did insist that that vision of love was grounded in God himself and not an "optional" conclusion of human reasoning.

7. The Christian vision of a community in which all are

"friends of God," a community in which the neighbor's good determines one's conscience, a community free from social hierarchy and partiality, can never be a community in which "love of enemy" or respect for social order is adopted as the strategy of weakness, as a "slave morality." Christians do not act out of a feeling of powerlessness but out of a conviction that love represents the presence and power of the Spirit.

8. Finally, the images of eschatological salvation reside in the Christian community as it struggles to learn love and experiences forgiveness. They do not apply simply to individuals. Nor is the love command addressed to isolated individuals. The individual cannot be asked to "love the enemy" independently of a community of "brethren" which supports him/her, that is, a community that loves and aids those whose witness may exact a high price from them.

SELECTED BIBLIOGRAPHY

Berger, K.	*Die Gesetzesauslegung Jesu. Teil I: Markus und*
1972	*Parallelen.* WMANT 40. Neukirchen-Vluyn: Neukirchener.
Betz, H. D.	"De Fraterno Amore" Mor 478A–492D, *Plu-*
1978	*tarch's Ethical Writings and Early Christian Literature.* SCH IV. Leiden: Brill, 231–46.
1979	*Galatians.* Philadelphia: Fortress.
Bogart, J.	*Orthodox and Heretical Perfectionism in the Johan-*
1977	*nine Community.* Missoula: Scholars.
Bornkamm, G.	"*Das Doppelgebot der Liebe,*" *Geschichte und*
1968	*Glaube I.* (Gesammelte Aufsätz III). München, 37–45.
Bowker, J.	*The Targums and Rabbinic Literature.* London:
1969	Cambridge.
Brown, R.	*The Gospel According to John. I-XII.* New York:
1966	Doubleday.
1970	*The Gospel According to John. XIII-XXI.* New York: Doubleday.
1970	*The Community of the Beloved Disciple.* New York: Paulist.
Brown, S.	"The Matthean Community and the Gentile Mis-
1980	sion," *Novum Testamentum* 22:193–221.
Bultmann, R.	*Theology of the New Testament I.* New York:
1951	Scribner's.
Caird, C. B.	*The Language and Imagery of the Bible.* Philadel-
1980	phia: Westminster.
Carlston, C.	"Reminiscence and Redaction in Lk 15:11–32,"
1975	*Journal of Biblical Literature* 94:368–90.
Conzelmann, H.	*1 Corinthians.* Philadelphia: Fortress.
1975	

Crespy, G.
1974

Crossan, J. D.
1973
1974

Davis, C.
1980
Derrett, J. D. M.
1967/68

Dibelius, M. &
Greeven, H.
1976
Fichtner, J.
1955

Fisher, J. A.
1978
Freyne, S.
1980

Fuller, R.
1978

Funk, R.
1974
Furnish, V.
1968
Göppelt, L.
1978
Grundmann, W.
1971
Harrelson, W.
1975

Hollander, H. W.
1975
Horsley, R.
1978a

"The Parable of the Good Samaritan: An Essay in Structural Research," *Semeia* 2:27–50.
In Parables. New York: Harper.

"The Good Samaritan: Toward a Generic Definition of Parable," *Semeia* 2:82–112.
Theology and Political Society. London: Cambridge.
"Law in the New Testament: The Parable of the Prodigal Son," *New Testament Studies* 14:56–74.

James. Philadelphia: Fortress.

"Der Begriff des Nächsten im Alten Testament," *Wort und Dienst.* Jahrbuch der Theologie Schule Bethel. NS 4:23–52.
"Ethics and Wisdom," *Catholic Biblical Quarterly* 40:298–310.
Galilee: From Alexander the Great to Hadrian. Wilmington: Michael Glazier/Notre Dame: Notre Dame.
"The Double Commandment of Love: A Test Case for Authenticity," *Essays on the Love Commandment.* Philadelphia: Fortress, 41–56.
"The Good Samaritan as Metaphor," *Semeia* 2:74–81.
Theology and Ethics in Paul. Nashville: Abingdon.

Der Erste Petrusbrief. Göttingen: Vandenhoeck & Ruprecht.
Das Evangelium nach Matthaus.[2] Berlin: Evangelische Verlagsanstalt.
"Patient Love in the Testament of Joseph," *Studies on the Testament of Joseph,* ed. G. Nickelsburg. Missoula: Scholars, 29–35.
"The Ethical Character of the Patriarch Joseph," *Studies on the Testament of Joseph,* 47–104.
"Consciousness and Freedom among the Corinthians: 1 Corinthians 8–10," *Catholic Biblical Quarterly* 40:574–89.

1978b "The Background of the Confessional Formula in 1 Kor 8,6," *Zeitschrift fur neutestamentliche Wissenschaft* 69:130–35.

1980/81 "Gnosis in Corinth: 1 Corinthians 8:1–6," *New Testament Studies* 27:32–51.

Houlden, J. L. *A Commentary on the Johannine Epistles.* New
1973 York: Harper.

1977 *Ethics in the New Testament.* New York: Oxford.

Jeremias, J. *The Parables of Jesus.* New York: Scribner's.
1963

Johnson, L. T. *The Literary Function of Possessions in Luke-Acts.*
1977 Missoula: Scholars.

Jonas, H. "Seventeenth Century and After: The Meaning of
1980 (1974) the Scientific and Technological Revolution," *Philosophical Essays: From Ancient Creed to Technological Man.* Chicago: Chicago (Midway), 45–80.

Karris, R. "Poor and Rich: The Lukan *Sitz im Leben,*" *Per-
1978 spectives on Luke-Acts,* ed. C. Talbert. Association of Baptist Professors of Religion, 112–25.

Kaesemann, E. *Commentary on Romans.* Grand Rapids: Eerd-
1980 mans.

Kee, H. "The Ethical Dimensions of the Testaments of the
1977/78 XII Patriarchs as a Clue to Provenance," *New Testament Studies* 24:259–70.

Küng, H. *Does God Exist?* New York: Doubleday.
1980

Lietzmann, H. *An die Korinther.*[4] Tübingen: J. C. B. Mohr (Paul
1949 Siebeck).

Machovec, M. *Jesus fur Atheisten.* Berlin.
1972

MacRae, G. W. "The Fourth Gospel and Religionsgeschichte,"
1970 *Catholic Biblical Quarterly* 32:13–24.

Meier, J. *The Vision of Matthew.* New York: Paulist.
1979

Metz, J. *Faith in History and Society.* New York: Seabury.
1980

Murphy-O'Connor, J. "1 Cor viii, 6 Cosmology or Soteriology?" *Revue
1978a Biblique* 85:253–67.

1978b	"Freedom or the Ghetto (1 Cor VIII 1–13, X 23–XI 1)," *Revue Biblique* 85:543–74.
1979	"Food and Spiritual Gifts in 1 Cor 8:8," *Catholic Biblical Quarterly* 41:292–98.
Mussner, F. 1967	*Der Jakobusbrief.*² Freiburg: Herder.
Niederwimmer, L. 1968	*Jesus.* Göttingen: Vandenhoeck & Ruprecht.
Perkins, P. 1978	*The Gospel according to John.* Chicago: Franciscan Herald.
1979	*The Johannine Epistles.* Wilmington: Michael Glazier.
1981	*Hearing the Parables of Jesus.* New York: Paulist.
Piper, J. 1979	*Love Your Enemies.* London: Cambridge.
Sampley, J. P. 1980	*Pauline Partnership in Christ.* Philadelphia: Fortress.
Schillebeeckx, E. 1980	*Christ.* New York: Seabury.
Schlier, H. 1965	*Der Brief an die Galater.*⁴ Göttingen: Vandenhoeck & Ruprecht.
1977	*Der Romerbrief.* Freiburg: Herder.
Schnackenburg, R. 1965	*The Moral Teaching of the New Testament.* New York: Herder.
1968	*The Gospel according to St. John. vol 1: chs 1–4.* New York: Herder
1970	*Die Johannesbriefe.*⁴ Freiburg: Herder.
1975	*Das Johannesevangelium III. Kap. 13–21.* Freiburg: Herder.
Schottroff, L. 1978	"Non-Violence and the Love of Enemies," *Essays on the Love Command,* 9–39.
Schurmann, H. 1969	*Das Lukasevangelium I Kap. 1.1–9,50.* Freiburg: Herder.
Smith, C. W. F. 1975	*The Jesus of the Parables.* Philadelphia: Pilgrim.
Stendahl, K. 1962	"Hate, Non-Retaliation and Love," *Harvard Theological Review* 55:343–55.
1976	*Paul among Jews and Gentiles.* Philadelphia: Fortress.

Suggs, M. J.
1978

"The Antitheses as Redactional Products," *Essays on the Love Command,* 93–107.

Tolbert, M.
1979

Perspectives on the Parables. Philadelphia: Fortress.

Via, D.
1978

The Parables. Philadelphia: Fortress.

Walker, W. O.
1978

"Jesus and the Tax Collectors," *Journal of Biblical Literature* 97:221–38.

Ward, R. B.
1966

"The Communal Concern of the Epistle of James," Unpublished Th.D. Dissertation. Harvard University.

1968

"The Works of Abraham Jas 2:14–16," *Harvard Theological Review* 61:283–329.

1969

"Partiality in the Assembly: James 2:2–4," *Harvard Theological Review* 62:87–97.

Whittaker, J.
1979

"Christianity and Morality in the Roman Empire," *Vigiliae Christianae* 33:209–25.

Winston, D.
1979

The Wisdom of Solomon. New York: Doubleday.